INDIA'S
EX-UNTOUCHABLES

*the text of this book is printed
on 100% recycled paper*

BY HAROLD R. ISAACS

The Tragedy of the Chinese Revolution

No Peace For Asia

Two-Thirds of the World

Scratches on Our Minds: American Images
of China and India

Emergent Americans: A Report on Crossroads Africa

The New World of Negro Americans

India's Ex-Untouchables

American Jews in Israel

As Editor

New Cycle in Asia

Straw Sandals: Chinese Stories, 1918–1933

As Contributor

As We See Russia

South Asia in the World Today

The Urban Condition

Communication and Propaganda in World History

INDIA'S

EX-UNTOUCHABLES

HAROLD R. ISAACS

HARPER TORCHBOOKS

HARPER & ROW, PUBLISHERS

NEW YORK, EVANSTON, SAN FRANCISCO, LONDON

A Study from the Center for International Studies,
Massachusetts Institute of Technology.

A hardcover edition of this book was first published by M. W.
Patwardhan at Sangam Press Private Ltd., and by P. S. Jayasinghe,
Asia Publishing House, Bombay, India, in 1965. It was originally
published in hardcover in America by John Day Company in 1965.
It is here reprinted by arrangement.

INDIA'S EX-UNTOUCHABLES.

Copyright © 1964 by Harold R. Isaacs.

Copyright © 1965 by Massachusetts Institute of Technology.

First HARPER TORCHBOOK edition published 1974.

STANDARD BOOK NUMBER: 06–131737–3

They alone rise who strive. Some of you nurse the wrong notion that you will not rise in this world. But remember that the age of helplessness is ended. A new epoch has set in. All things are now possible....

—B. R. Ambedkar, in a speech to a meeting of Untouchables in Bombay in February, 1933.

PREFATORY NOTE

——————————— ✿ ———————————

I went to India early in 1963 to find out what has been happening to educated ex-Untouchables in these first years of Indian independence. I use the term "ex-Untouchables" because Untouchability has been abolished in India by law, if not in fact. My inquiry was a modest one and so is this report in which I simply pass on what I learned from talking with some 50 individuals going through this experience: students, teachers, civil servants, professionals, politicians, who have come up through the openings in Indian society created by the new educational opportunities of these years. My brief report obviously does not exhaust the subject, but it does introduce it. This is a good enough reason alone to make it available in this form. There is also the connection between the experience of Untouchables in India today and that of Negroes in the United States. I have had to resist the temptation to turn this report into an examination of all the parallels and non-parallels, but I expect they will tug hard enough by themselves at every reader's mind while he discovers, probably for the first time, some of the features of the Indian part of this story.

These and other comparisons remain, however, very much

part of my own task, for this report covers only one of a series of explorations made during this year in an effort to learn something more about the interaction between political change and group identity. This has to do with the ways in which changing systems of political power are compelling many different kinds of people to change the ways in which they see themselves and in which they relate to others. People everywhere are being forced to rearrange the elements of their group identities in order to meet their rearranged circumstances. In the great disorderly tangle of human affairs, new racial, cultural, and national identities are being formed in a nearly universal reach for new sources of self-respect. My present set of inquiries into examples of this experience follows some of the matters opened up in *The New World of Negro Americans*, published in 1963. I pursued them in an exploratory way in Israel, India, Malaya, the Philippines, and Japan, and other examples elsewhere still beckon. Each separate inquiry turns up its own further glimpse of some new feature of this changing human story and I have learned that one sees more through small apertures than through large. So there will first be further reports and then the time will come for the comparisons, for an examination of the nature of group identity and its relationship to politics and power systems on the one hand and the well-being of the individual on the other, especially as reflected among young people who have lived all their lives under the impact of great social and political change.

This work of inquiry is being done on a grant from the National Institute of Mental Health. For their supporting interest in this whole undertaking, I have a special acknowledgment to make to Dr. Benson R. Snyder of M.I.T. and Dr. Leonard J. Duhl of N.I.M.H. For help of many different kinds in the making of this particular inquiry in India, I have to thank Dr. Dhirendra Narain of the University of Bombay;

Dr. B. Kuppaswamy and the late Dr. Kali Prasad of the International Centre of New Delhi; Mr. L. P. Singh of the Home Ministry; Mr. Vimal Chandra, Assistant Commissioner for Scheduled Castes and Tribes; Hon. B. S. Murthy, Deputy Minister for Community Development; Hon. B. Rachiah, Minister of Forests in Mysore, and his aide, Mr. M. N. Chikkaiah; Mr. Minoo Masani, M.P.; Principal H. R. Karnik of the Siddarth College of Arts and Sciences in Bombay; Mr. L. B. Manikatti of the Mysore Department of Social Welfare; and to every one of the dozens of others who received me so hospitably and joined me so fully and generously in exploring the questions with which I came to them. I have also to thank Prof. Myron Weiner of M.I.T. for some bibliographic counsel, Miss Enid Bok for her extremely useful M.I.T. seminar paper, "The Scheduled Castes in Indian Politics," and Mrs. Laura Farnsworth for her competent secretarial assistance. None of these individuals has any share of the responsibility, obviously, for how I have used what they have helped me to learn.

I am not sure about burdening her also with responsibility, but just about every other part of this enterprise has been shared to a decisive extent by my co-worker, co-investigator, co-interviewer, co-hort, and co-exister-in-chief, Viola R. Isaacs.

H. R. I.

Cambridge, Mass.
October 21, 1964

*A substantial portion of the material
in this book first appeared in somewhat
different form in* The New Yorker.

CONTENTS

INTRODUCTION

———————————— ✿ ————————————

Just after midnight Easter Sunday morning in 1963, we were driving back from a Bombay suburb and as we left the posh seaside neighborhood and moved through the streets of thickly packed shops and tenements that make up most of this crowded city, we came on small groups of people gathered outdoors around brightly lit altars, Christian groups holding Easter morning services. Around a curve nearing the Bandstand downtown, we came upon a dark, silent, unlit crowd of several hundred grouped around the statue of B. R. Ambedkar, the late great leader of India's Untouchables who died aged sixty-five in 1956. At the statue—a larger-than-life-sized figure with finger raised, the gesture of earnest exhortation in which he so often appeared before his followers—a Bombay Fire Department truck was maneuvering a ladder cautiously close to the bronze head. A single searchlight played on it as the crowd stood silently watching. When the ladder was inched up to within reach, a member of the group clambered up, carrying with him a tangled heap of tinseled garlands. With the help of a fireman and a firehook he finally managed from his precarious perch to drape the garlands around the statue's head. A cheer went up. The crowd began to applaud

and to shout slogans having to do with downing the rich
and upping the poor. Then up front someone began to intone
a prayer. With their singsong responses, the crowd became a
Buddhist congregation. Near the end of his lifelong struggle
to lead the Untouchables to a better lot, Ambedkar had despaired of ever winning a decent equality within the fold of
Hinduism and a few months before he died led some 300,000
of his own group, the Untouchable Mahars, in a mass conversion to Buddhism. Through these same streets half a million
people thronged in his funeral procession, and a hundred
thousand of them embraced Buddhism in a ceremony at the
crematorium. Ambedkar has since been semi-deified by his
followers. Lights burn at the base of his statue, which has
become a place of worship, and his picture hangs in home
altars where, like pictures of Gandhi and Nehru among the
gods in many Hindu homes, it is regarded with prayerful rev-
erence. This night's ceremony was in observance of the an-
niversary of his birth. The fire truck had backed away from
the crowd which barely filled the small plot of ground on
which the statue stood. The prayers and the singing ended, a
new round of slogans was shouted, and the meeting came to
an end. The traffic rounding the circle stopped, pausing
for curious looks. The small band of poorly dressed faithful
melted away in the warm darkness into the surrounding
streets.

The next morning I attended an even smaller memorial
gathering at Siddharth College, which Ambedkar founded in
1946 and which is now housed in several large shabby
buildings in downtown Bombay. Several caste Hindu members of the governing board of the college and its sponsoring
body, the People's Education Society, were present along with
about a hundred students and members of the staff out of a
school body of some 2,500. Prayers were first said in the
entrance hall, first on one side under a garlanded portrait

of the Buddha, and then on the opposite side, under a similarly garlanded portrait of Ambedkar. From there we moved down a hall lined with pictures of Newton, Voltaire, Einstein, and Shaw, to a large lecture room where a tall scholarly man, one of the visiting caste Hindu dignitaries, reminded the group that the Untouchables were "the most despised section of all humanity." He warned the young people in front of him not to build a personality cult around Ambedkar. He told them Ambedkar would not want them to worship him but to work to see that hundreds and thousands of new Ambedkars rose among them. "If you really want to honor Ambedkar," he said, "decide that you are not going to be just another yielder to power, or a tool of power. Aspire to be another Ambedkar, decide to struggle against injustice, and give your life to it." It was an earnest speech and the audience of neatly dressed young men applauded politely, and then everyone went into the next room where cake and fruit and tea were served. Here I arranged with members of the staff and some of the students to explore further with them what it meant now in India to be an ex-Untouchable moving along the newly widened channels of education and opportunity to some new kind of view of oneself and a new kind of life.

Of all the many different kinds of people in the world going through transforming experiences of this kind, certainly few have to reach up from as far down as the ex-Untouchables of India to arrive at some more bearable minimum share of the common life and a more tolerable group identity for themselves. There are nearly 65,000,000 of them, the greater mass of them still bogged in the morass of Indian village life. But while static backwardness remains the condition of most of them, great changes have come for some. There are about 4,000,000 ex-Untouchable children now in primary schools, about 1,500,000 in middle and high schools, and 55,000 of their young people are in the colleges and universities—with something like 2,800 of them emerging each year with bachelor's degrees—and at various educational levels large numbers are moving into government jobs, most of them in the lower clerical grades. I knew I could only hope to get a brief glimpse of the experience of people going through this process of change, but even in a glimpse, I found, there was a great deal to see when nobody had ever looked that way before. Even some quite knowledgeable friends and associates to whom I mentioned my plans had looked a bit incredulous, and it was clear that in their minds' eyes, Untouchables were still illiterates living in rural squalor—which most of them indeed still are—and that none of them had yet acquired any mental picture of city-dwelling middle-class Untouchables wearing white shirts and trousers and speaking English just like so many other educated Indians. Few, to be sure, were much higher than very low middle class, and very few had moved anywhere within reach of the upper, cosmopolitan circles where most foreign contact is made. But educated ex-Untouchables are quite visible in Indian life now and easily discoverable for anyone who seeks them out. What I know about them now I know from some rather doggedly difficult digging at several ministerial offices in New Delhi for some of the "large" items of information, mostly statistical, and for the rest from some 50-odd interviews, mostly with ex-Untouchables, standing at various points along the path of change.

Seeking out these individuals, I found myself dealing with more than one generation, for the process of education and change of status now taking place somewhat more rapidly for much larger numbers under the government of independent India had actually begun much earlier under the British. Those I spoke to included several politicians of high rank, one of them a member of Nehru's cabinet, another a deputy minister, several senior civil servants, several Members of Parliament—by now their ages have dropped into the thirties —a number of much more junior government officials, several university faculty members, including one young woman with an English Ph.D., a young man who is about to win his Ph.D. at an Indian university, a large assortment of M.A.s and LL.B.s, a lady doctor with the English-style medical degree called M.B.B.S. (Bachelor of Medicine and Bachelor of Surgery) and her lawyer husband, and down into the twenties, several dozen university and college undergraduates. I heard of several remarkable top-achievers who were ex-Untouchables, including the winner of a double first from Cambridge now serving abroad in the Indian Foreign Service, and I met one, a young man whose father was an illiterate agricultural laborer, who himself has become a pilot for Indian Air Lines. My wife and I also had a glimpse of the beginning of this educational process, at a tiny nursery school in a remote corner of Mysore, where tots of three or four are taking the first step out into the new world of the classroom under the wondering eyes of their illiterate parents and grandparents, whose seamed faces lined the windows on the day we visited the school. We had a close-up look at a village and some brief talk in the sun with some of the ex-Untouchables in front of the hovels in which they lived at the village edge. We visited the ultra-slums of Bombay where a great mass of ex-Untouchables are now, as in other cities, the lowest among the urban lowly. Although we conducted our inquiry only in New Delhi, Bombay, Bangalore, and Mysore, we had the good fortune to talk with individuals from seven different Indian states and belonging to about a dozen different ex-Untouchable "castes" or "communities."

Out of these assorted encounters in a brief space of time, we were able to glean some idea of what had been happening to these individuals and to their community. As modest as these gleanings necessarily were, they seemed to add up to new knowledge of the subject. I found that government officials most intimately concerned with the affairs of the ex-Untouchables were able to provide information about what the government was doing but had no information at all about the effect of these programs. By 1963, for example, the number of scholarships (which in India are stipends for maintenance) given by the central government for ex-Untouchables in colleges and universities had risen to the substantial figure of 55,000 but no one had any information to show how these students were performing, how many were falling by the wayside, how many were finishing and winning degrees, or how many degree-winners were winning first- second- or pass-class degrees when they did finish. It seemed to be difficult enough to dispense all this educational opportunity without adding the task of trying to discover the results. The office of the Commissioner for Scheduled Castes and Tribes in New Delhi had, I found, circulated an inquiry to all state governments asking for some information along these lines. That was in 1961, and up to mid-1963, not a single reply had ever come in.

It also did not take long to discover that the problem of the ex-Untouchables was all but entirely ignored in the circles of politicians, intellectuals, journalists, writers, and scholars where I had some friends of many years standing and to whom I went now with some of my inquiries. This was partly because India has a host of problems, all enormous, all overwhelming, and men can spend lifetimes struggling with them without ever coming into touch, so to speak, with the problems of the ex-Untouchables. "Yes, I know," said one friend who had grown old in the effort to help modernize India, "I know this is an important problem, but it never enters our lives." India too has its invisible men. This is partly a mirror of the fact that with rare individual exceptions, ex-Untouchables have not yet made their way into the environments of the middle or upper levels of society. Hardly any caste Hindu I asked could name a single ex-Untouchable he knew or even knew of, aside from the two or three highly visible top politicians who are professional ex-Untouchables. Part of the explanation is perhaps suggested by a prefatory remark in a recent book on Indian rural problems by a well-known woman writer, Kusum Nair. "Caste and Untouchability," she observed, "are not normally mentioned in polite society." One reason, she added, "is often the fear of being misquoted or misunderstood by foreigners." Another reason was suggested to me by an Indian psychiatrist who said: "There is an enormous amount of make-believe in the way Indians deal with problems of life." I ran into some examples of this. "We are all one." Or: "This sort of thing has disappeared in the cities." Or: "The upper class doesn't care about caste anymore!" At a dinner party of very cosmopolitan people one night I raised the question, asking whether anybody had a Scheduled Caste acquaintance. There was a blankly uncomfortable negative all around, but one woman recovered quickly, exclaiming: "But then, how would I know—we never know what a person's caste is!" Her husband would not go along with this. "No," he said, "if anyone in my circle of acquaintances was of the Scheduled Castes, I'd *know* it!" Bits of truth hide in this fog, but it is mostly fog, and very little was being done by anybody to clear it away. In the academic sphere, I could discover only the most fragmentary indications of research touching on this subject. One of India's top anthropologists and authorities on caste told me there was so much to do on other aspects of caste that he had not been able to deal except in a peripheral way with the problems of Untouchability. He could not name any scholar who had taken this as his special field of interest. It was suggested to me that caste Hindu scholars tend to stay away from the subject and no one else, least of all ex-Untouchable scholars, approaches it. The lady Ph.D. I met in Mysore had done her thesis research in a village of her own district but had studied some other aspect of village relationships, and a candidate for a degree in sociology quite clearly thought his best course was to avoid dealing directly with the subject that concerned him most. "The truth is there are no Harijan intellectuals," said a former university professor who had been interested in this area for a long time and to a most unusual degree. "Those coming up now simply become teachers," he added, "and they remain in the safe and traditional fields."

I found in general in my talks with caste Hindus that almost any statement about these matters was subject to contradiction from one authority to the next. In fact, each individual authority usually managed to contradict himself about it several times over in a single conversation. This was not necessarily because of any deliberate attempt to obfuscate or conceal but because the facts themselves are really confused and are different from place to place, and also because there is an absolutely vast ignorance shared by everybody about what is actually going on. I found that after talking to about 50 educated ex-Untouchables in the course of a month, I had actually talked more and had more contact with such individuals than all but two or three of the caste Hindus whom I had sought out for information in the course of my inquiry. I found that like the caste system itself, the status of Untouchability still governed the lives of those affected by it and that the small number of those who have been able to move up and out of the mass and away from the worst of it move into that peculiar semi-limbo reserved for men in motion between two identities. They are forever picking their way among seen and unseen obstacles, many outside and many inside themselves, as they try to cut loose from the huge mess of attachments and rules of life which hold them strongly bound no matter what they do or where they get to, for Indian society is simply not changing fast enough to provide them with enough new and open ground onto which they can freely move. Little as I have learned about the people now going through this experience, it appears to be more than anybody else has reported, and this is reason enough for setting it down.

INDIA'S
EX-UNTOUCHABLES

1. *THE UNTOUCHABLES*

Untouchability goes back into the far dimness of the Hindu past. Like so much else in Hindu history and practice, origins remain vague or unknown, interpretations contradictory, and opinions controversial. But there is nothing vague about caste or about Untouchability itself. This system for elevating and debasing human beings in rigidly separated compartments developed as the actuality of Hindu life while Hindu philosophy was holding itself to be the most open and all-inclusive of all ways of thought, the Hindu religion the most tolerant of any on earth. The great abstractions of universal all-in-oneness filled the vast empty space around its philosophic peaks while an intricate system of separations and exclusions took shape down the creased valleys and out on the great plains where human beings actually existed and formed their societies. The 65,000,000 people officially described as belonging to the Scheduled Castes in India now comprise just under 15 percent of the total population according to the 1961 census. In other words, one out of every seven Indians belongs to this category, ex-Untouchables by law but in their greatest mass over most of the country still Untouchables in fact.

By ancient and holy writ (especially the Manusmriti, or the Laws of Manu, which Ambedkar once publicly burned in a bonfire that seared much of Hindu India), the Untouchables were marked off as people whose touch pollutes and elaborate regulations were established governing the conditions of their

25

separation from the rest of the people. Hindu holy writ is like all other holy writ in that it can be and has been quoted in every possible direction on the same subject. There are passages establishing merit and righteous conduct, rather than accident of birth, as the basis for locating a person's proper place in society, but as at least one Indian scholar has bluntly put it: "Any acquaintance with the caste system in practice goes to show that the ethical aspect of caste is mere talk and has nothing to do with the actual facts." [1] The Untouchables were set apart outside and below the four main divisions of Hindu society, the Varnas or castes of priests (Brahmins), warriors (Kshatriyas), merchants (Vaisyas), and servitors (Shudras). These large groups broke up into masses of sub-groups, all with intricate sets of rules and regulations governing their contact with each other; but there is a major line dividing the top three Varnas from the fourth, the Shudras. The top three are entitled to wear the "sacred thread" which identifies them as "twice-born"—meaning that in a symbolic second birth they have been admitted to the study of the Vedas or, in effect, recognized as more or less fully privileged Hindus. At the present time the people belonging to these three large caste groups in India total about 90,000,000, or about one-fifth of the population. Below them are the Shudras, the "once-born," who by Hindu tradition are forbidden to share in knowledge of the holy writings or any of the other benefits of the religion—apparently including at one distant time even the "right" to hope for better status in an actual second birth through reincarnation. The Shudras were present to serve the upper castes, so while they were kept low they were also kept touchable. In today's India the members of the Shudra castes are numbered at some 250,000,000, more than half the total population.

[1] A. R. Wadia, "Working Paper," *Report of the Seminar on Casteism and Removal of Untouchability*, Bombay, 1955, p. 5.

Still another large and distinct element is the tribal and hill peoples now numbering about 30,000,000, some of whom are Hindus and some not, but who, however backward they may be, are still touchable in Hindu terms. The Untouchables, however, are Hindus who are kept outside the Hindu pale, while remaining remarkably subject to Hindu sanctions and rules governing their lives. There are conditions fixing permissible contact between high order and low right through the Hindu system, but only the Untouchables were placed beyond all touch at all times. It is this Untouchability, according to the noted Indian scholar G. S. Ghurye, that marks the Hindu caste system from all others, past or present. Set apart to perform needed but ritually impure functions, the Untouchables also performed that peculiarly useful function in any society of occupying the bottom, that bottom of the bottom where mere lowliness—such as that suffered by the Shudras—was underpinned by a condition that was clearly subhuman. This was hard on those elected to be the subhumans but helpful to the Shudras, no doubt, and to everybody else on up the line.

As the system added refinements over the dim ages, the Untouchables were also made Unseeable, Unapproachable, Unhearable. The details are frequently Unbelievable. In many places they could not enter at all upon streets or lanes used by caste Hindus, or else they had to carry brooms to brush away their footprints in the dirt behind them as they passed. In some places they could not contaminate the earth with their spittle but had to carry little pots around their necks to keep the ground reserved for caste Hindu spittle only. In one southern region, there were prescribed distances that Untouchables had to keep from the different levels of upper caste people, 33 feet from the lowest-rated group, 66 feet from a second middling caste, and 99 feet from the Brahmins, the highest-rated of all. By some rules an Untouchable had to shout a warning before entering a street so that all the holier folk could get out of the way of his contaminating shadow. By others he could not raise his voice at all because the sound of his voice falling on a caste Hindu's ear was deemed to be as polluting as his touch. Some rules fixed the manner of house he could live in, the style of dress or undress he had to use—in some parts of South India until well past the middle of the nineteenth century, Untouchable women could not wear any clothes above the waist, and in some places even today nothing resembling ornament or finery is allowed. In many areas Untouchables could not have music at their own private festivals, such as weddings. They could not enter any Hindu temple, caste Hindu house, or other establishment, or take water from the common village well.[2] The Untouchables, cut out of the community altogether, served—and largely still do serve—as its scavengers and sweepers, the handlers of the carcasses of its dead animals whose flesh they eat and whose skins they tan, the carriers of waste and night soil, the beggars and the scrapers, living in and off the dregs and carrion of the society. Besides this they perform a good part of the plain ordinary toil of the fields. At one point in some parts of the country some sage Hindu landholders decided that the work of *digging* was also ritually impure and therefore below their sacred dignity and a task to be passed on to landless laborers kept under strictest control. Today ex-Untouchables are 42 percent of the landless laborers of the country. They live not only beyond this spiritual pale in religiously sanctified exclusion, but also beyond a physical wall as well, dwelling now, as from time immemorial, in their rigidly separated living quarter, always the most miserable and squalid quarter of India's 700,000 villages. The 65,000,000 people now officially called the "Scheduled Castes" are scattered out across the country, minorities of 10 to 18 per-

2 Cf. Ghurye, *Caste and Race*, Bombay, 1932, pp. 8–13.

cent in most of the states, and slicing down into smaller and smaller groups in each district and village, always a small minority in each unit.

This dispersion by numbers, moreover, is further fragmented by deeply cleft divisions and subdivisions among the outcasts themselves. In a formidable demonstration of the universal law by which the dominated ape the dominators, the Untouchables split up like the touchables into their own "castes" and "sub-castes," appearing in separate groups and grouplets in every state, region, district, village. It is obvious that the Indians who charged the British with dividing and ruling were heirs of past masters of the art. The official list of the Scheduled Castes, first published by the government in the early 1930's and revised and reissued by the Government of India in 1957, shows, as far as I can make out, that there are about 1,100 of these "castes." Some of these recur in different states or regions, sharing the identity attached to a common occupation and sometimes a common name, and I was told that if one consolidated the government's listings by these similarities, the total would become 405. But in their greater mass, these remain separate and distinct groups, each with its own name, its own particular slice of the tradition of pollution, its own set of ritually impure tasks to perform, its own local set of rules to observe, its own different local master caste not to contaminate. But this is not all. In a further example of how far the debased can go in internalizing their debasement, many of these Untouchable groups proceeded to practice various degrees of Untouchability among themselves and against each other. In the manner of the touchable castes up above, members of many of these submerged groups will not eat together or take water from each other or allow intermarriage. These writs still run strong among the ex-Untouchables in India. Even today intercaste marriage is apparently rarer among the outcasts than it is among the touchable

Hindus. Untouchabilit\` among ex-Untouchables is still strong enough in many villages to become a serious additional obstacle—alongside caste Hindu intractability—in the path of government programs, like building wells, intended to eliminate such caste practices altogether.

The origins of this system are a continuing matter of speculation among scholars and there are clearly more theories than facts in what one can read now in the works of the contending authorities and interpreters.[3] The most commonly repeated version is that it all dates back to prehistoric times, perhaps four or five thousand years ago, when otherwise unidentified "Aryan" invaders made themselves the masters of the indigenous population they found in the land now known as India. From the relationship between conqueror and conquered established in that dim time came, it is alleged, the relationship between upper and lower castes in India today, with the Shudras associated with the subjugated people of that prehistoric time, and the Untouchables with some lower-than-low separation that was made at the bottom of the social scale. There is a matter of skin color involved here also although it, too, like everything else, has been blurred through time, ignorance, and controversy. The word "varna" or "caste" actually means "color" and it has often been said that the "Arya" were "fair" and the "Dasa" or "Dasyus," the local people, were "dark." [4] In Vedic times, up to about 600 B.C., the authorities say, the conquered people were called "the dark people." The Dravidian people of southern India were, and still largely are, a black or dark people, and these differences are the sources of a sometimes-virulent modern "Aryanism" among some Indians. In any case, the protective

3 Cf. Ghurye, *op cit.*, pp. 61, 142ff; also Wadia, "Working Paper," *loc. cit.*, pp. 1–10; cf. B. R. Ambedkar, *Who Were the Shudras?* Bombay, 1946, and *The Untouchables*, New Delhi, 1948.

4 Ghurye, *op. cit.*, pp. 41–2, 46–8; Wadia, *loc. cit.*, p. 4.

system of exclusions and separations for the Brahmins and other upper castes presumably began as a way of solidifying and maintaining power over a conquered mass and there is some suggestion that the first Untouchable groups emerged from forbidden and strongly tabooed mixing between the high and the low. It seems likely enough that the "purity" the Brahmins tried to maintain was not merely ritual and not only political but also racial.

These differences are traceable in Indian society today although the racial lines could not remain as distinct as the caste lines proved to be over such a long period of time. You now have a range of skin color among Indians from quite fair northerners to quite black southerners; and there is a distinct, even a blatant, set of color attitudes among many Indians, as the matrimonial ads for "fair" brides in any Sunday paper will illustrate. But these color differences seem to slice only irregularly into the patterns of the touchable and the Untouchable. It is frequently said that the Untouchables are darker-skinned and a biographer of Ambedkar refers to his dark brown color as one of his handicaps in life. An ex-Untouchable from Kerala, in the south where both caste and color distinction are sharply held, told me that the choice insult used by caste Hindu children against Untouchable children was *"karupan"* ("black fellow") or *"karupi"* ("black girl"). It is certainly true that the ex-Untouchables I met or saw were almost all of the darker rather than the lighter side of brown. But there are black or near-black Brahmin southerners and there are certainly lighter brown Untouchable northerners and perhaps even some who are "fair." In any case, while color has a role in it, the line of pollution and Untouchability is clearly not a color line. Generally the ex-Untouchables one meets share all the varieties of physical appearance one finds among caste Hindus from region to region. Some of the suggested distinctions were

more of a class nature than racial. One individual told me
he could always recognize Mahars in Bombay as "dark," but
also as "rough-skinned" or "rough-handed" people who also
spoke in an uncouth manner. Given all the varieties of Indian
darkness, poverty, roughness, and uncouthness, none of this
was evident to my no-doubt unschooled eye, but I thought
my informant was merely reflecting to me his own image of
the lower orders. I do not know whether one would ever
encounter an ex-Untouchable who looked anything like the
fine-featured Brahmin Nehru, but there are certainly millions
of caste Hindu Indians who look as dark and as roughly hewn
as the darkest and most roughly hewn ex-Untouchable. If all
the touchables and Untouchables were reshuffled and somebody tore up the caste scorecards, no one—at least on the
score of physical appearance—could tell them apart.

The mark on these people is not physical but social, traditional, religious, and psychological. Traditional Hindu doctrine held that they were born to their condition or fate
(karma) because of sins committed in an earlier life. If they
submitted faithfully and performed their duty (dharma) without complaint in this life, they might—not surely, but only
might—hope for a better life the next time around. Ambedkar
pitted himself against his people's belief in this doctrine.
"Your humiliations are a matter of pride with others," he
told them in savage wrath. "You are made to suffer wants,
privations, and humiliations not because it was preordained
by sins committed in your previous birth, but because of the
overpowering tyranny and treachery of those who are above
you. . . . Do not believe in fate. Believe in your strength." [5]
Ambedkar became one of modern India's most famous men
as a result of his struggle to break down the Hindu caste
system, but he made hardly a dent in it; and he was followed

    [5] Quoted by Dhananjay Keer, *Dr. Ambedkar, Life and Mission*, Bombay,
1962, p. 233.

not by the great masses of Untouchables scattered all over the country but only by a part of his own community, the Mahars of Maharashtra, the region in which Bombay is situated. Despite new laws and some earnest reform efforts by some caste Hindus, the caste system, which Ambedkar saw as the heart of the matter, stands in many ways stronger than ever. Traditional Hindu practices have given way only a little, more rapidly in the cities than in the villages, but nowhere has the system begun to crumble. Great masses of legal ex-Untouchables are still Untouchables not only in fact but in their own minds, living, as a top ex-Untouchable politician once said, "in psychological cages," [6] remaining much like the old man of whom a Brahmin writer friend told me. This old man, an Untouchable, stood outside the gate of his home when he came back from school one year, a youth all fired up with enthusiasm for India's emancipation from its dead past. "Come in!" the boy urged the old Untouchable. "Come in the house!" The man stood there and looked at him with a stern eye. "*You* may have given up your religion, young master," he said, "but *we* have not given up *ours*."

[6] Address by Shri Jagjivan Ram, *Report of Seminar*, p. 29.

2. *THE NAME TO GO BY*

In writing about ex-Untouchables in India it is needful to begin to clear up the knotty question of the name they go by. Here, as always, there is a great deal indeed in the name. To begin with, there is no general name of common acceptance that actually describes this large group of people. I have chosen to use "ex-Untouchable" as the most precisely descriptive term that can be applied at this time to people whose past names are no longer usable or acceptable and who hope in the future to need no special name for themselves at all. The dreamy vision of India's struggling nation-builders is that all the thousands of names by which people group themselves in India—by caste, by language, by region—will eventually be superseded by the single common name "Indian" in which all will meaningfully share. The sense of this new common identity still flickers only fitfully among the peoples of India, and I met some ex-Untouchables who would eagerly reach for it if it would only become strong enough and inclusive enough to meet their great need. Unfortunately it is still far from doing so. Right now ex-Untouchables do not know what to call themselves for they are people trying to cease being what they were and to become something else, though they are not sure what. As a result, all the names they now go by are matters of conflict and ambivalence and reflect in various ways their history and their status during this time of change.

I had noticed that in his writings, B. R. Ambedkar usually referred to his people simply as "Untouchables," that the

official term for them was "Scheduled Castes," and that a third
term in frequent use in the literature on the subject was
"Harijan." From the very first conversations I had with anybody on the subject in India, certain nuances of usage quickly
became apparent. The term "Untouchable" had disappeared
from ordinary parlance; it was not only impolite to use it
but illegal. The new Indian Constitution of 1949 legally
"abolished" Untouchability. There is no such thing legally as
an "Untouchable" in India. I also began to note that the term
"Harijan" was used freely in the main not by ex-Untouchables but by caste Hindus. Very rarely would an ex-Untouchable use it about himself, though it might flicker through his
talk in some general connection. I also noticed that while it
might be used to this extent by a supporter of the Congress
Party, it was never used at all by the much smaller group of
supporters of Ambedkar politically organized in the Republican Party. In both cases they would much more commonly use the term "Scheduled Caste" both as noun and
adjective, e.g., "He is a Scheduled Caste person" or "I am
Scheduled Caste." This phrase, pronounced in variations of
"she-dool'd caste," has grown less awkward with usage but has
hardly acquired the sound of a name.

Except for the stark word "Untouchables" there never was
any single name to cover this great mass of people. In the
various Indian languages they were known by many versions
of words that mean "Untouchable" or "outcast" or variations
thereof: Pamchamas, Atishudras, Avarnas, Antyajas, Nama-
shudras, etc. One also comes on "Pariahs," "Unseeables" and
"Unapproachables." In British officialese sometime late in the
last century the term "Depressed Classes" was introduced and
remained the most commonly used, though vague, name of
the group for many decades. In 1919 the first separate representation on a number of public bodies was given to members
of the "Depressed Classes" and this included Untouchables

along with quite a scatter of others, such as the aboriginal
Tribes. It was not until 1932 that the term "Depressed
Classes" was officially defined as meaning only the Untouchables. But it was just about at this time that "Depressed
Classes" was replaced by "Scheduled Castes." This came about
because the British government, already engaged in a number
of programs for the benefit of this lowest group, was preparing
to include it in the array of communal separate electorates
(for Muslims, Christians, Anglo-Indians, etc.) through which
it hoped both to appease and to weaken Indian nationalist
pressure. Special effort was made in the 1931 census and by a
special committee to draw up a "schedule" of the "castes"
entitled to benefit from these various special arrangements.
At the Round Table Conference in London in 1931, held to
discuss future political concessions by the British in India,
Ambedkar demanded a separate electorate for the Untouchables and he also made a special demand for "a change of no-
menclature." He proposed that the Untouchables be called
"Protestant Hindus" or "Non-conformist Hindus." [7] What
emerged instead, when the electoral award was made and
eventually incorporated into the Government of India Act
of 1935, was the new official term "Scheduled Castes."

At this point the matter of the name gets entwined with
some crucial history and the role of Gandhi in relation to
Untouchability. Gandhi had said from the beginning that it
was one of his aims to purge Hinduism of Untouchability.
Indeed, at the outset of his career in Indian politics in 1920,
he declared that *swaraj* or self-government would be "un-
attainable without the removal of the sins of Untouchability."
He saw this as a reform to be brought about by exhortation
and example. In his own *ashram,* or retreat, he and his im-
mediate entourage demonstratively cleaned their own latrines

<hr>

[7] B. R. Ambedkar, *What Congress and Gandhi Have Done to the Untouchables,* Bombay, 1945, p. 317.

as a symbolic way of "cleaning the Hindu society," and Gandhi also adopted an Untouchable girl as a daughter. He saw Untouchability as an "excrescence" or an "appendix in the body of Hinduism" which had to be removed, leaving the rest of the caste system intact and purified. Gandhi preached on this persistently enough to disturb some of his caste Hindu followers, but Ambedkar charged him with being weak and equivocal at best in his pursuit of this aim. "How can [Untouchables] believe," he asked, "in the earnestness of a man who does nothing more than indulge in giving sermons on the evil of Untouchability?"

The difference here was a fundamental one, for while Gandhi attacked Untouchability and not caste, Ambedkar argued that the heart of the problem of Untouchability was the caste system itself. 'There will be outcasts as long as there are castes," he held. "Nothing can emanicipate the outcasts except the destruction of the caste system." This was a view also held by some Congress liberals and radicals, including Nehru, but not by Gandhi, who wanted Hindu society to put an end to Untouchability and revert to the original system of four Varna, or large caste divisions, of the distant past. Although he long exhorted his fellow caste Hindus to give up sinning against the Untouchables, very little effect was ever given to his plea and he never directly forced the issue upon them. He saw it as a matter for long and patient correction and as a "lesser" issue within the "greater" one of freedom from British rule. Ambedkar was unwilling to accept either Gandhi's conception of the problem or his timetable. "There have been many Mahatmas in India whose sole object was to remove Untouchability and to elevate and absorb the Depressed Classes," Ambedkar said at the height of the 1932 crisis, "but every one of them has failed in his mission. Mahatmas come and Mahatmas have gone. But the Untouchables have remained as Untouchables." Hence Am-

bedkar sought political guarantees and political power to en-
sure they would be honored. To this end he sought and won
a separate electorate for the Untouchables in the new arrangement with the British. Gandhi, who reluctantly accepted the
political separateness of the other groups as a "necessary evil,"
absolutely opposed any grant of separate political power to
the Untouchables. This would permanently sever the Untouchables from the main Hindu body, he said, and this he
would not accept either as a matter of religion or of politics.
He thereupon proclaimed a "fast-unto-death" to force revi-
sion of the electoral award. Ambedkar argued that the Untouchables were and always had been "separate" from the
main body of Hinduism and that only separate political power
would win for them rights that caste Hindus would never
voluntarily yield to them. He observed bitingly that Gandhi
never embarked on a fast to force caste Hindus to abjure the
practice of Untouchability but did so now to keep the Untouchables from getting a share of the power for their own.
For more than a week as Gandhi lay fasting in Yeravda Prison
in Poona, the uproar raged around Ambedkar's head, the
Congress press charging that he had made himself the tool of
a British plot to divide-and-rule. In the negotiated outcome,
which became known as "the Poona Pact," Ambedkar yielded
up the "separate electorate" which he won in the award, and
accepted in its place a system of reserved seats for Untouchables under a "joint electorate" with the caste Hindu majority.
This arrangement had the air of also being a concession by
Gandhi—who had originally opposed any kind of special political representation for the Untouchables—but it had the effect,
as events later showed, of keeping the legislative representa-
tives of the Untouchables under the effective controlling influence of the dominant Congress Party.[8]

[8] The authoritative Gandhian account of these events is given in Pyarelal,
The Epic Fast, Ahmedabad, 1932, and is reflected in the account given by

Following the fast and his pact with Ambedkar, Gandhi
spurred his campaign among caste Hindus to mitigate the
evils of Untouchability and there was a brief spurt of response
among some of his followers, mainly in the form of temple-
openings which were reported for a time with great acclaim
from week to week in the Gandhian press. (Ambedkar,
who had little use for temple entry if it was not linked to a
fundamental assault on the caste system, commented scorn-
fully later that most of the temples opened "were dilapidated
and deserted temples which were used by none but dogs and
monkeys." Over a celebrated temple entry issue in 1933,
Gandhi threatened to fast, but did not do so.) It was in the
course of this campaign to promote improvement and uplift
for the Untouchables that Gandhi bestowed on them the new
name, "Harijan," a word meaning "children of God" which he
took from a poem by a sage in his native Gujarat. His "Anti-Un-
touchability League" became the "Harijan Sevak Sangh"
and he started a publication called *Harijan*. The new name
was intended, it was said, to give new dignity to the Untouchables and to impress on caste Hindus the need to admit these
unfortunates into the Hindu fold.

Gandhi's caste Hindu followers adopted the new name and

Louis Fischer, *The Life of Mahatma Gandhi*, New York, 1950, pp. 306–321 and
similar works. Ambedkar's record appears in *What Congress and Gandhi
Have Done to the Untouchables*, Chap. III and *passim*, and additional details
giving Ambedkar's view will be found in his biographer's account in Keer,
Dr. Ambedkar, Life and Mission, pp. 204–216. Of the Untouchable legislators
elected as a result of the Poona Pact, Ambedkar later wrote: "They were
completely under the control of the Congress Party Executive. They could
not ask a question which it did not like. They could not move a resolution
which it did not permit. They could not bring in legislation to which it
objected. They could not vote, as they chose and could not speak what they
felt. They were as dumb as driven cattle. One of the objects of obtaining
representation in the Legislature for the Untouchables is to enable them to
ventilate their grievances and to obtain redress for their wrongs. The Congress
successfully and effectively prevented this from happening."—*What Congress
and Gandhi Have Done to the Untouchables*, p. 102.

it evidently soon passed into common usage among them.
I have no way of knowing how it was among the Untouchables
themselves in the beginning, but I do know that now it never
takes long in any conversation with the most committed Congress Harijan to discover that he does not really like the term
and by choice avoids it.[9] Back in 1938 on one occasion
Ambedkar's group in the Bombay state assembly challenged
the Congress majority on this issue. They demanded that the
term "Harijan" as used in a bill then before the House be
changed to "Scheduled Castes." The chairman, a Congress
caste Hindu, replied that he thought the name was intended
to give dignity to the Untouchables and challenged Ambedkar to suggest a better name. "Ambedkar replied [re-
corded a biographer] that all he would say was that he was
not in a position to suggest any better name." [10] When the
Congress majority voted them down on the subject of their
own name, Ambedkar and his followers walked angrily out of
the chamber.

In my own talks with ex-Untouchables I was given more
than one reason for the discomfort felt, even by Congress
followers, over the term "Harijan." A former member of
Parliament and one-time member of the Gandhi entourage
said:

We usually don't use the word "Harijan." In fact, most educated people don't like "Harijan." The word connotes Untouchability and I don't think anyone likes it. Before Gandhi introduced
it we were simply known as the "Untouchables," or by particular
group names, such as Mahar, Mala, Pulaya, and so on. But very
few liked to be called "Harijan." Nobody took it in the right

[9] In 1955, Jagjivan Ram, the Congress Party's highest ranking ex-Untouchable as Minister of Communications in the Nehru cabinet, gave a
major address on the subject of Caste and Untouchability without ever
once using the term "Harijan."—See "Address by Shri Jagjivan Ram,"
Report of Seminar, etc., pp. 25–39.

[10] Keer, op. cit., pp. 301–302.

spirit. Gandhi wanted to remove the inferiority and give a sense of superiority. But people did not take it that way. It just meant getting another name instead of a caste name, but a name that meant the same thing: Untouchable.

A graduate student from Andhra described himself as a follower of Congress but said: "I do not like 'Harijan.' It means 'children of God.' Aren't all the other people children of God too? Why this particular name for us? I think it is very childish." The followers of Ambedkar, who have now shrunk in the political sphere to the tiny Republican Party with just five members in the lower house, are rather more colorful in their explanations. One of these members of Parliament gave me this crisp version:

"Harijan" is a bad word introduced by Mahatma Gandhi. In Hindi it means a boy whose father's name is unknown, hence "children of God." In the Hindu temples there were, as you know, the devadassi, the girls who took part in worship ceremonies and also served the priests. Sometimes they gave birth to children and these children were called "Harijan." That's why we don't like the name.

While this seemed to leave the unwieldy "Scheduled Castes" as the nearest thing to an accepted general name, I soon gathered that ex-Untouchables much more commonly referred to themselves, or thought of themselves, by their various "caste" or "community" names. But these too were a constant reminder of status. In the home village—still "home" even to most of those who have become city dwellers—the caste name itself was usually used by the caste Hindus as a derogatory expletive. " 'Chamar' is a word carrying contempt," said a Chamar from the Punjab, now a senior civil servant in New Delhi. "In school other children called us 'Dhor' as a way to dismiss us with contempt," said a young woman, a Dhor, who is now a physician in Bombay. The

twenty-seven-year-old son of a prominent politician from
Andhra remembered from his childhood some of the feelings
surrounding the attempt to get rid of the shame of the group
name by using Gandhi's recently bestowed substitute:

I came to know (from my father) that the word "Harijan" was
for Malas and Madigas. I think at that time people like my
father following Gandhi found it easier to say "I'm Harijan"
than to say "I'm Mala." It was hard to say you were a Mala. I
was in the 6th standard when the teacher asked me what caste
I was. I said: "I'm Harijan." The whole class mocked at me
when I said that. All the heads turned as though to look at a
convict. I felt ashamed, embarrassed, and looked down on.

His younger brother, now twenty-three, returned to that
village a few years later—the family was living in Madras
then but he would come back with his mother at vacation
time. He discovered the shame of being "Mala" not from caste
Hindu boys but from Madigas, another Untouchable group
in the village which had located itself above the Malas and
practiced some degree of Untouchability toward them:

Those boys called me "Mala!" and said: "Don't talk to him,
don't touch him!" The first time this happened, I must have
been five years old or so. I went to my cousin, my father's nephew,
and I asked him: "What is Mala?" He told me we belonged to
the Mala caste. The next time I was called Mala I kept quiet.
I didn't get annoyed. I just kept quiet. I would feel bad and go
away. My cousin had not explained it all to me but I knew it
was very low ... I never asked anybody about this. I assumed to
myself this was the rule of society and we are all subject to the
rules. When I went to someone's house, I would be asked what
caste I was. When I said "Mala" I had to stand outside. Naturally
one feels this. Having stayed in Madras, I felt it very bad to be
in a village of mud huts where they made you stand outside.
I wanted to run away, I felt insulted, and I wanted to run, but I
didn't run.

Here is a boyhood recollection of a man of fifty who is a Paravan from Kerala:

My father's name was Kunjen and he would be called Kunjen Paravan. I was called Velu Paravan. The name Kunjen Paravan was not derogatory to my father but Velu Paravan was quite derogatory to me. I would not allow myself to be called this to my face, because I did not want to be called by my caste name which signified backwardness. . . . At school no caste names were allowed but the other boys still used it and I would quarrel or fight whenever I was called Velu Paravan. If we got into a fight, they would begin to call me by my communal name. They could call me "Paravan" but there was nothing I was allowed to say that could relate to their caste or group or their father's name. We were not allowed to call other groups by their names. We could only address others as "Acha," which means "sir" or "father." We could only use this term of respect. Even now in the village an old man would have to call even a caste Hindu child not by his name but by "Acha." But even a caste Hindu child could address my father as Kunjen Paravan. In this way the group name itself became an insult. The term "son of a Paravan" or "son of a Pulayan" [another Untouchable group] were all bad names. For someone simply to say "You are a Pulayan" was to call a bad name. The upper caste children used these names to insult us.

Thus the caste name itself became the common term of contempt and shame whenever it was used by others and could hardly avoid carrying this freight with it whenever one used it to identify oneself. For older people who stayed in the villages this had been and largely remained the accepted state of things. For the youngsters now going to school, it soon became a fighting matter. For the educated ex-Untouchable who went out into the world to go to more advanced schools, or those who came up in the big city and encountered these humiliations whenever they traveled out in any direction, it became the source of a constant harassment of spirit.

Although it is now frowned upon by more cosmopolitan Indians and it happens much less often now than it did in the big cities, the practice of asking a person to identify his caste is still a common practice for great masses of people in everyday life in India. For the educated ex-Untouchable, this common occurrence has become a maddening challenge to his conscience and his self-respect. If he answers truthfully when he is asked, he may still more often than not be denied a job, a place to live, a bed to sleep in, food in a restaurant, coffee or tea at a café, even a drink of water. On trains and buses especially, it seems, a frequent and familiar opening gambit of conversation is: "And what community do you belong to?" Each person has to devise his own way of meeting this question. If an ex-Untouchable tells the truth in reply, he is likely to feel, almost like physical impact, the sudden fall of silence in the crowded compartment, a pulling away from contact, a cutting off of further talk. "When I travel anywhere I am upset and discouraged by this," said a Master of Arts from Gujarat. "I have learned that if people you are travelling with know you are Scheduled Caste, they would never offer you water or a place to stay, and this is true even today. So I never declare my community or my name. Nobody among us does. We never talk about community, because the mentality of the people hasn't changed."

Among the Mahars I met in Bombay there was always the double edge to the dilemma; whether, if they chose to identify themselves at all, to say "Mahar" or "Buddhist," though the effect in both cases would be the same. A person would want to assert his aggressive rejection of Hinduism and say boldly "Buddhist!" while knowing that he would catch at once that quick glassy look in the other's eye and almost hear the thought clicking in his mind: "Oh, Buddhist-Mahar-Untouch-

able keep away!" One individual told me the effect was much
the same if one said "Christian," even though the conversion
of Untouchables to Christianity in any significant numbers
goes back a long way. One young man, with some malicious
enjoyment, told me that he always turned a cold gaze on his
questioner and said severely: "And *why* do you want to
know?" This had a freezing effect, he explained, because
very often the question of caste would be put to a well-
dressed and obviously educated young man by a fellow
traveler on the lookout for a suitable husband for his daughter
or other relative. In such cases, the cold answer was usually
enough to reduce the questioner to embarrassed silence.

It was, of course, best when no one asked and no answer
had to be made at all, no identity acknowledged. In most of
the daily comings and goings of urban life nowadays no one
does ask this question very much anymore—except, that is,
when it has to do with getting into school, qualifying for a
job or getting hired, getting a place to live, getting married,
or in the affairs of life surrounding a birth or a death. In
the great common namelessness of crowded city streets or
public places, there is respite. But to be engaged on any of
the important business of life, to be traveling anywhere, to
be mixing with people casually on trains or buses—to be in
any of these situations is to face the still-recurring question:
what community do you belong to? For most Indians it is
still the most important question to ask a man, while for the
ex-Untouchable it is the question above all that he does not
want to answer.

Some of the same weight is attached also to personal names.
Traditionally an Untouchable had no surname but would be
known by a given name and after it, for further identification,
the given name of his father. Indeed, by this tradition also,
Untouchables did not choose their children's names; this was
the prerogative of one's landlord or employer in the village,

or some other local caste Hindu dignitary. This would often simply be whatever day of the week it happened to be. Thus if you were born on a Tuesday in a Hindi area, your name might be "Mangala." Often caste Hindus would give the name of some lowly object, also an unclean one, like "Panahi" which means simply "shoe." Often they might bestow what were called "bad" names, such as a word which literally means "a person who should be dragged." Now, educated ex-Untouchables more usually do the naming themselves and of course they choose "good" names, which I gathered means Sanskrit-sounding names taken from among those used by the touchable castes, not uncommonly the name of some god, hero, or benefactor. Among the ex-Untouchable students I met in Bombay, I found a remarkable number of them all with the name "Gaikwar" and was puzzled by this until I learned that this was the family name of the Maharajah of Baroda, who opened early opportunities for Untouchables in his realm and gave Ambedkar his chance for higher education abroad. There were also quite a few named "Shinde" —the name of a caste Hindu reformer in Maharashtra who had taken up the cause of the Depressed Classes around the turn of the century. But other names would be chosen mainly for their good upper caste sound, "good" names like the recognizably Brahmin Pande, Mehta, or Parshad, a Banya name like Vakil or Patel, a Kshatriya name like Singh (which could be either a Sikh or a Rajput name) and their equivalents in other language areas.

The choice of names has become part of the process of shedding the old identity and acquiring a new one. Sometimes this is quite literally a way of blotting out one's identity in order to "pass" as a member of some higher caste. But while for some the choosing of new names is a way of trying to erase the past, for a few it is a way of making a demand on the future. One of the small group of Ambedkar's successors in Parliament, a self-assured and roughly handsome young man of thirty-six from Uttar Pradesh, told me: "I have four children: a boy of eight whom I named Ajai, which means a person who can never be defeated; a girl of five I have called Anula, after a famous Buddhist princess of Ceylon; a son of three I named Kennedy because he was born in 1960, Kennedy's year; and the youngest boy, only five months old, I have named Lincoln."

3. THE EX-UNTOUCHABLES

Untouchability was declared "abolished" by Article 17 of the new Indian Constitution of 1949, a charter largely drafted by Ambedkar as Law Minister in Nehru's first post-independence cabinet. The practice of Untouchability was declared "forbidden" and "punishable in accordance with law." The Untouchability (Offences) Act of 1955 spelled out many of the particulars and fixed penalties for infractions. It established the legal right of former Untouchables to enter Hindu temples and to draw water from public wells and streams, to have access and use of every kind of public facility, including shops, cafés, restaurants, hotels, hospitals, housing, all forms of transportation, to wear whatever kind of clothes they wished or enter any occupation they desired. Penalties of imprisonment and fines were laid down not only for anyone who obstructed the exercise of these rights but used "words, spoken or written" that might have an obstructive effect.

The waving of these legal wands obviously did not cause Untouchability to disappear. This was going to take a rather thoroughgoing renovation of the entire society to put an end to a system of inequality practiced and sanctified by holy writ for several thousand years. The difficulty may be gauged by considering what it has taken in the United States to achieve even as much legal wand-waving in a society where all sanctity was attached to doctrines of equality of status, and respect for all men had theoretically been in effect since the birth of the Republic. In India you do run into a few individuals who out of ignorance, self-deception, or some need to deceive others, do declare that Untouchability has been in fact "abolished" in India. More commonly one is assured that it is "really disappearing," that "it is really not very important, and in any case, who cares about caste anymore?" As I have already observed, it was invariably a caste Hindu who made statements of this sort, usually a caste Hindu who rather fancied himself as a member of the cosmopolitan elite, and who very much wanted to wish this matter away by ignoring it. I did not meet a single ex-Untouchable, however, who thought that Untouchability was disappearing or that caste was less important now than it used to be in India.

"There is an amazing complacence among the intellectuals in the country and among the educated community in general," wrote L. M. Shrikant, a caste Hindu who devoted himself to this problem for ten years as Commissioner for Scheduled Castes and Tribes. "Our efforts have largely been confined to platitudes, publicity, and propaganda which are hardly adequate to shake the roots of this evil which has persisted throughout the period of India's recorded history." [11] Shrikant's report is filled with evidence of the stubborn persistence of the evil. The nation "has made some progress," it says, but this "is more or less confined to urban areas.... Rural India has not evinced much change in this regard." In the state of Uttar Pradesh, for example, "the practice of Untouchability continued unabated." Spot checks in various provinces showed that despite their legal rights, ex-Untouchables were still being excluded from temples and public places, still being denied a cup of tea in cafés, still being refused service by dhobis (washermen) and barbers,

11 *Report of the Commissioner for Scheduled Castes and Tribes,* 1960–61, New Delhi, p. 26.

who are themselves among the lowest castes though touchable. The 1960–61 Report contains, for further example, this unhappily blunt passage:

The government of Rajasthan [one of the states of India] have reported that cases of Untouchability are not very common and there is only infrequent observance of Untouchability at public places. This is not at all correct, as according to our information, Rajasthan is one of the few erstwhile feudal areas where Untouchability and other social disabilities are practiced in the worst, even violent form.[12]

In the catalogue of reported infractions, one finds charges that a caste Hindu in an Andhra village had let his cattle graze on an ex-Untouchable's field and had gone unpunished, that in Bihar a group of ex-Untouchables had been refused permission to participate in a public ceremony "because they would pollute the deities of the high caste people," and a report from a town in Gujarat, Gandhi's home province, where some ex-Untouchables "were beaten by caste Hindus as the former had used music instruments at a marriage ceremony." A sociologist at the University of Bombay and his assistant gave me a note listing some of the conditions they had found the previous summer applying to the Vankars, an ex-Untouchable caste of weavers, in the Gujarat village of Alali:

If Vankar children by chance touch any of the Baria [the local upper caste] children in school, they are punished or turned out of class; if a Baria approaches, they must move to the other side of the road and give way to him; they cannot enter the temple; they cannot fetch water from the well the Barias use; they must stand at a distance from the Barias; the harassment has actually increased in the last few years with increased im-

12 *Ibid.*, p. 29.

poverishment; educated boys cannot wear good or clean clothes without inviting bad comments from the Baria.[13]

The Report of the Commissioner for Scheduled Castes for 1961–62 showed that a total of 2,898 complaints had been filed with the police under the Untouchability (Offences) Act since its passage in 1955, but that fewer than a third of them had been disposed of in the courts, and some were still pending after six or seven years. "As pointed out in previous reports," the account said, "the number of cases registered under the Act by itself can hardly be taken as an index of the incidence of Untouchability. Due to their economic dependence on caste Hindus, the Scheduled Caste persons concerned generally do not risk approaching the police, who also, it is reported, do not at times properly register the cases reported to them." [14]

There are various programs for the welfare, uplift, and improvement of the lot of ex-Untouchables in India. They are mostly bogged down in the terrible inertia of a vast and backward society that has responded only fitfully so far to the new regime's efforts to change it. There is a program for distribution of land to the landless laborers, nearly half of whom are ex-Untouchables, but this has not had spectacular success up to now. There are plans for new housing for the ex-Untouchables and a few such housing projects have been carried out in a number of places—we saw a few of them when we traveled in Mysore, modest brick houses that were palaces compared to the old mud hovels more commonly seen everywhere in the villages. These improved houses were just as separate from the villages as the old quarters had been

13 From a note supplied by Prof. A. R. Desai and Uday Mehta, University of Bombay, April 1963.

14 *Report of the Commissioner for Scheduled Castes and Tribes*, 1961–62, p. 8. A later figure supplied by the office of the Commissioner in August 1964 brought the total number of cases reported to 3,776.

and have given rise to the charge that the government has been perpetuating segregation of the ex-Untouchable instead of promoting integration. In any case, as official reports all wearily acknowledge, none of this has moved very far or made much of a dent in the general condition.

Somewhat more has been accomplished to improve the water supply, a problem for everyone in India and especially in rural India. A major item in the community development program has been the supply of new sanitary wells to the villages. The ex-Untouchables in the villages have generally been denied the use even of the old unsanitary wells that some villages had, and this has presented the improvers with grievous choices. It has often become a choice between giving the poorest of the village poor access to some kind of decent minimum water supply or else hewing to the line of struggle against Untouchability and letting them continue without good water. The official report says that in many places instead of insisting upon common use of the new wells, the government has constructed "separate drinking water wells for the Scheduled Castes." The report goes on: "This no doubt provided drinking water facilities for the Scheduled Castes to a certain extent, but this step has not been helpful in the removal of Untouchability." But there is worse still. Forced by caste Hindu intractability to dig extra wells inside the Scheduled Caste locations, the servants of government reform have often run into the problem of Untouchability among the Untouchables. "In certain areas," the report says, "this prejudice is so strong that separate wells have to be provided by the government for different classes of Scheduled Castes living in the same village. This fact weakens"—the report adds rather plaintively—"to some extent the campaign for the removal of Untouchability." [15]

But perhaps the welfare program that most vividly illus-

[15] *Report of the Commissioner*, 1961–62, p. 7.

trates the nature of the problem and the kinds of backwardness that have to be overcome is the program undertaken by the government to improve the lot of the scavengers. The lowest of all tasks in this lowly society is the removal of night soil and this has traditionally been the task of Untouchables at the bottom of even the Untouchable scale. This kind of scavenger is known as a *Banghi* and the Banghis are a people apart even among people apart. The 1951 census showed some 3,500,000 people working as scavengers, sweepers, and drain cleaners in India, more than half of them working in urban areas. This was the group whose lowliness Gandhi tried to raise, at least in reputation, by leading those who lived with him to clean their own latrines, an example followed by a few aspiring saints but not by the people at large. Gandhi interested himself in the problems of the technique of night soil removal as one way of improving the dignity of the task and this is something which his welfare group, the Harijan Sevak Sangh, and various government agencies have tried to pursue in the years since Indian independence. "The practice of carrying night soil as head loads by scavengers and sweepers is widely prevalent throughout the country," says the Commissioner's Report for 1960–61. To end this "degrading practice," a scheme was advanced in 1957–58 to help municipalities and other local bodies provide scavengers with wheelbarrows to use for this purpose instead of the buckets or baskets they had been using. Money was granted but there seems to have been considerable difficulty in getting the localities to use it. Of a total of R9,000,000 ($1,890,000) supplied for this purpose through 1962–63, only R5,300,000 ($1,100,000) was actually expended. This was partly lethargy, partly a generic disinterest of caste Hindu officials in special efforts needed to improve the lot of the ex-Untouchables. But it was also partly something else. The change, it seems, was not very popular among the scavengers themselves. "Most of the scavengers are women [says the government report] [16] and they feel that wheelbarrows are difficult to ply and that it is more convenient to carry the night soil in baskets as head loads or on the waist." The report urged "tactful handling" and suggested that the wheelbarrows "should be light and durable." But the weight and shape of the wheelbarrow was not the only problem. Wheelbarrows were useful on this job only if they could "be taken right up to the latrine [and] in most towns there are narrow lanes where wheelbarrows cannot ply easily." Therefore the municipality "should wherever possible widen the lanes so that the wheelbarrows can be carried as near as possible to the latrines and the receptacle emptied therein." But neither would providing light wheelbarrows nor widening the lanes quite solve the problem, for the report goes on stolidly to say: "It has been estimated that in about 80 to 90 percent of latrines, there are no receptacles and human excreta drops directly on the ground and the scavenger has to remove it. . . . It is therefore essential [to] insist that proper receptacles must be used in all private and public latrines." It is further pointed out to the municipalities that after all this is done, the wheelbarrows themselves cannot be allowed to remain filthy, so it is necessary to provide places "where the wheelbarrows can be washed and properly parked after the day's work is over."

But neither is this the happy ending. Even if there are receptacles, wide lanes, light wheelbarrows, and places to wash and park the wheelbarrows, the problem is not quite licked, for "in many states it has been observed . . . that some latrines have very small openings for removal of receptacles, necessitating the scavenger to bend and insert the upper part of his body while cleaning them." At this point the report concludes that what really needs to be done with all these installations is to abolish them. It ends up by

[16] *Report of the Commissioner*, 1960–61, pp. 303ff.

urging that all public places be provided with "flushout latrines... connecting them to an underground sewage system." To all of this the report adds that something must also be done about 1) the private contractors who in most places hold the night-soil-removing concessions and stand between the municipality and the scavengers and 2) about the localities that misuse or misdirect the funds given to them for these purposes. You can start, in sum, with the idea of providing a scavenger with a wheelbarrow but you end up not only having to rebuild your towns and cities with modern construction and sanitation but also having to make over the social system while you are at it. The scavenger's lot is clearly not a happy one but whoever would change his lot has to shoulder the whole burden of Indian backwardness—while the scavenger himself (or herself), far from seeking any changes, would more likely than not just let things stay as they are.

In Bombay I came upon a footnote to this subject. The city employs about 20,000 ex-Untouchables in its conservancy, or sanitation department. They pursue their traditional occupations though some of them are able to do it in somewhat modernized versions. They are the city's collectors of trash and garbage as well as the keepers of its streets. Very few of them have moved into the more skilled occupations that have become part of this work in modern Bombay. None have become mechanics, for example, but some have become drivers. I met a young Brahmin named P. G. Joshi, a young man with a high brow and a heavy black beard, who invited me to visit him at the large truck depot he manages for the conservancy department. "We have about 500 drivers," he told me as we looked down from his office on the busy yard. "About 200 of them are Mahars and 150 Kathywarris, another Scheduled Caste group from Gujarat. The rest are Marathas [caste Hindus] and Muslims and others. They all drive

trucks collecting refuse or moving gravel for street construction and so on. Most of the city has underground sewage now
but there are ten localities which have no sewers but where
they use cesspools instead and we have the job of pumping
them out into tank trucks. The Marathas and the Muslims
drive on all jobs except the cesspool jobs, and the same goes
for the Mahars. They will drive garbage trucks but they won't
go in as cleaners of cesspools. They will not touch jobs connected with cesspool cleaning. That's why we have the Kathywarris—they're the only ones who'll do the job for us."

The changes that have come in the cities are partly a
product of the new laws, partly a natural consequence of the
burgeoning cosmopolitanism of modern urban life, especially
the anonymity pressed by any great city on its masses of
people. In the crowds that fill the streets, jam the trams and
buses, use the shops, stalls, and the public places, no one
ever asks who is what. The ex-Untouchables who fill the
bottom slot as the poorest of the city poor still largely carry
on with their traditional occupations, but significant numbers
of them do shift to labor in factories, to work on the railways,
to become bus drivers and the like. Except for the thin
upper crust that has risen to places in middle-class neighborhoods, and the larger cut of lucky ones who have rooms in
the blocks of houses or colonies provided by the various
government agencies, the great mass still lives in its own
separate neighborhoods. In Indian cities, people of a kind
huddle together even more than they do in cities elsewhere
in the world and there are usually fairly well-defined quarters
where the different castes and groups tend to cluster and self-
segregate themselves. In this arrangement of areas, all of
them poor, most of them slums, the ex-Untouchable locations
are always at the lowest level of urban squalor, which in
India is pretty low and pretty squalid. Only a very small

number of ex-Untouchables make their way out of these hovels to the comparative luxury of some of the great sprawling lower-middle-class tenement blocks that fill so much of a city like Bombay; and although "no one ever asks about caste in the cities," the ex-Untouchable who gets into one of these apartments usually does so by concealing his caste or even by falsifying it. The experience of Untouchability still waits for them at every turning of their everyday lives. Every ex-Untouchable I met had personally experienced Untouchability, whether in its traditional forms or in some of the new shapes of the new time, whether they were in their fifties or their twenties, whether in the village or in the city or while traveling between them. There have been changes, but nowhere, city or country, is it yet possible for such a person to live without being reminded constantly of his status or his lack of it.

Traditional Untouchability still persists in the village, and the links between city people and their country kin are still characteristically strong, even in families whose migration to the city took place a generation or even two generations ago. Many of the young people I met had been born in the villages and had come to the city as youths to pursue their higher education. Those born and raised in the city still went back with their parents to visit their country relatives and it was often on the first of these visits, when they were still small children, that they had their first soul-slaying encounters with the more brutally direct forms of treatment as Untouchables. These were all the more painful when, as in most cases, they had not been prepared for these experiences by their parents. The changing shapes of life for these individuals are vividly mirrored in their accounts of these early experiences.

Those who came up in the villages took in the facts of

life with the air they breathed. A lawyer-politician in his fifties said:

Our people's duty was to take away dead carcasses. They were not paid for this work and had to eat the flesh. This system is still found now, where people live on dead carcasses. They must also go to the houses of the caste Hindus and ask for bread, and the caste Hindus would throw out bread, half-chewed, dirty, rotten, and our people would mix this bread with the flesh and eat it. In my childhood I ate the food of dead carcasses and discarded bread.

A high-achieving young man in his thirties, who qualified for a Class 1 civil service post, remembered:

Right from your childhood you were aware of it. You couldn't touch others or go into their houses or take water from the well. If you wanted water, you begged for it, and if they were kindhearted, they would draw it and pour it into your pot. You were not allowed to take it yourself.

And a twenty-year-old undergraduate said:

In the village you learn your status. You know it by instinct. You begin to understand or get conscious of it, the separate localities for different groups, not being allowed to enter houses.

In some of these accounts of early years in the village you begin to pick up threads of some changing patterns. It can be as wispy as the knowledge that things could be different if only somebody dared, as a young man from Andhra said: "In our village it is rampant even now. It was and is still there. No change. Now Scheduled Caste people *could* go to the wells. *But nobody has tried it.*" In other accounts you begin to encounter parents who though they are still in the village are no longer illiterate scavengers and laborers but through modest schooling have become people of another kind. A particularly vivid and intense young man of twenty, a Siddharth undergraduate with bright flashing eyes in a smooth brown face, was full of his story of his village and his family, and he poured it all out in swiftly flowing speech, as though he feared I might disappear before hearing him out. He came from a village in the Dhulia district of Maharashtra where both his father and mother had become primary school teachers. His story about them suggests not only some of the terms on which change begins in the village but also that there may be more stirring than many realize as the influence of the small scattering of educated individuals begins to make itself felt. Here are the main parts of the story he told me:

I was in a field once where there was a well with a wall around it. I climbed the wall and looked down into the water. The farmer came up and slapped me because I was Untouchable. I knew this. It was the condition of our community. My father and mother never touched anything or anybody in the village. Other children had gone over the wall at the well. I just forgot and went to see what they saw. Once when I was a very small child and some of our caste people had eaten the flesh of a dead bullock, I asked my father: "Why are we Untouchable? Aren't we sons of the same god?" My father explained that some Mahars ate the meat of dead animals and were dirty and that was why we were Untouchable. My father and mother did not eat that kind of meat.

My father and other teachers in our district thought we must make progress and remove the reasons for Untouchability. He called a meeting of our people and it was decided that no one of our community would again eat the meat of a dead bullock, and that if anyone did, he would be fined five rupees. Some of our people soon broke this new rule and one of the men was fined five rupees. He refused to pay the fine, saying he did not have that much money. "I do not have five rupees," he said, "and I have nothing to eat. It is better to eat the meat of a dead bullock than to be hungry. It is the only way I can live." Then my father called another meeting and announced that *he* would take all the dead animals thereafter. Normally, a dead animal would be dragged away and the man who took it would skin it, sell the skin, and just leave the meat and the carcass for the rest of the people in the community in the village. When my father took over the task of taking away the dead animals, we dug a pit and put the carcass in the pit and closed it over. After nearly six months, we opened the pit, got the bones out and sold them. Together with the rest of the partly decomposed body, it was good fertilizer. After two or three years, some others in the community asked to take over that contract. It was good fertilizer and bones, easily sold. In this way there was no more eating of dead meat in our village and nobody has eaten such meat since then.

From another young man came a whole series of vignettes of changing levels in the village—literally levels because by the time he left the village for the city he could mount the stairs of caste Hindu houses, forbidden heights when he was a small boy. He also reflected the nearly universal experience of the village boy who comes to the city and for whom even the most squalid kind of ruralism can suddenly flicker with value that the city does not give. Listen to twenty-three-year-old Shinde, a good-looking, dark young man with a small moustache, a quick and easy smile, and a lively sense of the drama of his own experiences:

By the time I went to school in the village these things were not so hard and fast as when I was a smaller boy. I moved freely with other students but was still not allowed to enter their houses. Now we could climb the stairs to their verandas but could not go inside or drink water. Some people in the village would offer tea or water. When I was a boy no one did this, and it was very rare to go up any caste Hindu's stairs. In the family we were instructed: Do not touch. Do not go. Do not do this. Do not do that. They might get angry. You might get beaten. Better keep quiet.

I came to Bombay four years ago. It was my first time in a
big city. City life was an expanding experience. How people
behave! So different! Life is reserved. Nobody cares about other
people. Each one only cares about himself. In the village, if anything happens, people rush there. If someone dies or is married,
the entire village is associated with it. Here a marriage takes
place in the next hall and is over in an hour or so and nobody
notices it. In the village it takes a week! Here somebody dies
and nobody cares. In the village even when an old man or old
lady dies, everybody is there to perform or take part in the
ceremonies.

In the village there are the Scheduled Caste localities and here
too in the city, all living by groups, though side by side in a block
system. Nobody has contact with anybody else so nobody cares.
Here they don't ask what caste you belong to. If you go to the
village they are always asking, where are you from, what's your
name, what caste are you? Here they never ask. Here at school
I mix with all other students, with Brahmins, Bengalis, in the
hostel all kinds mix together, dine together. Nobody inquires
about it. The professors do not know the caste of the students.
They lecture for an hour and then go away. How would *they*
know? The students are mixed. If anyone knows or feels it, he
doesn't show it.

Of course they *do* feel it. They and we do have some superiority and inferiority complex, it is there. The Scheduled Caste
students know, but they are not courageous about it. They feel
we should not go and walk and talk with all those others. They
feel inferior and they do not mix. The others naturally feel
superior. But I always stepped out. I always stood first in my
class, even as a Scheduled Caste boy. I stood first, I felt, so it
was not necessary that I should remain behind!

It was easier for an ex-Untouchable youth to make the move
from village to city than for an ex-Untouchable child
to make the journey from city to village. Most of them did
make journeys like this because, as I have already remarked,
the family link remained close between those who had

migrated to the city and those who had not, and the distances were often not so great. (One young man raised in Bangalore told me you had to go into the "remote countryside" to find the old practices of Untouchability and when I asked him how far out this was, he replied: "Twenty miles.") One individual brought up in Bombay remembered when he first went back to the family village in Gujarat. "Our family lived in a separate area outside," he said "and you had to get permission to go inside the village. When you paid a shopkeeper, he would give you your change by dropping it in your shirt that you had to hold out so as to catch it. It was a humiliating thing." Another young man who had lived with his grandfather in Bombay until he was six had to go back to the village when his grandfather died and he too discovered his family's place "outside the boundary, behind the wall." He went on:

At noon or around eight o'clock at night, they used to go and beg for bread and food from house to house. One day my grandfather's brother, with whom we were staying, took me with him. I saw him begging and accepting what was given and I saw that I belonged to some different kind of community and that all were very, very poor. I asked my grandfather's brother why he begged. "In Bombay," I said, "we never begged." And he said, "This is our profession. We have to do it."

A man of forty, now on his way to high professional status, was haunted by his feeling of revulsion at his own kin. This came out of recollections like this:

When I went to the village, my maternal aunt gave us some food to eat. I found a mixture of pickles, bones, and pieces of vegetable, not a properly cooked dish. The rice was all mixed in with it, not separate. I asked her: "What is this?" She told me she had gathered it from the village people to give us, for we had come from Bombay as guests. From that day I thought of our people as beggars who had this way of avoiding starvation.

At marriage feasts, our people would gather around and loot the remains of the feast when it was over and they would fight and quarrel over them.

A Siddharth undergraduate, twenty-three years old, remembered this:

The village I went to with my mother is called Pachagaon. My grandmother is there. It was when I was eleven, in the 5th standard, and I had lived the free life in Bombay when I went to the village. On the way I asked my mother where I could get a drink of water. The home of a farmer was on the way and my mother asked the woman of the house for water. They did not give her water in a vessel but made us drink it out of our hands. I asked my mother why this was so. She said she would explain it, that it was due to the society which had these rules to separate superior people from inferior people. This was the first time in my life I had this experience. I felt bad. There seemed to me to be no difference between me and those people. But it was no use. It seemed to be our destiny.

Coming up in the city was a less charged experience, especially where the circumstances allowed a person to have a minimum of direct or personal contact with caste Hindus. These conditions varied, depending on the time and place. When he went to primary school in Bangalore, said a young man now twenty-six years old, he was not allowed to sit on a bench like the others, but had to sit on the ground. When he needed a haircut his father, an educated man and a civil servant, used to cut it for him because they could not go to a barbershop. "He explained to me that we had to be careful of caste Hindus." At the present time in the city of Mysore, a student has trouble finding a place to live.

When you go to a house to rent a room, the first question is, what caste are you? And when you say you are Scheduled Caste, they say, no rooms. Nobody rents to a Scheduled Caste person. The hostels are for rural boys and the regular hotels are too expensive. So I lived at home, quite a distance. At examination time, I took a room in a hotel, but I would not tell them my caste.

In bigger, busier Bombay, the Scheduled Caste population was more contained, and the neighborhood segregation provided its own insulation up to a point. One individual told me he went through the four primary grades in Bombay in a school where there were only Scheduled Caste boys. "It was not until after the fourth standard, when I was ten, that I ran into caste Hindus for the first time," he said, "and they avoided our company. The Scheduled Caste boys sat separately. We had our own benches."

The shift back and forth between city and village was a mixed thing, especially for an adult educated ex-Untouchable, and particularly if he had reached some assured respectable position. Such a person would sometimes be received back in his village with some respect, even by caste Hindu neighbors. He could enter their houses, this meant, and might even be offered tea, although this could never happen to any of the relatives he had returned there to visit. But perhaps the story that most acutely describes the present state of things comes from a Member of Parliament, a Chamar from Uttar Pradesh:

Once when I went back to the province and visited a village where there were caste Hindus, I found they were ready to sit and eat with me. I was very pleased with this. But when I came outside, I noticed a man of my own caste whom I had seen there before when I arrived. He was sitting out there waiting. I asked him why he was sitting there. He told me he had brought the *thali*—the brass bowl—and glass for me to use, and was waiting to get them back so he could go home.

4. THE FATHERS: EARLY EDUCATION

In the Laws of Manu, which date back nearly 2,000 years, it is ordered that molten lead be poured into the ears of any Shudra who dared to listen to a reading of the Vedas, the holy books. It is not clear whether by that time the Untouchables had already been sheared off from the lower rungs of the Shudra castes and driven into their total separateness, but obviously for them to presume to learn anything would have been an even greater sin. It has been said that despite this, the Untouchables did share a little in the oral tradition of Hindu lore and scripture, and there have even been some Untouchables poets and seers and holy men. But the plain fact is that these great masses of people were kept in all but total darkness generation after generation for many centuries. No hard facts about schooling for Untouchables appeared in the record until well into the nineteenth century.

The British role in this was a characteristic mixture of the pragmatic, equivocal, calculated, and philanthropic, with the proportions varying through time. In the early days the East India Company recruited Untouchables into its armed forces and provided them and their families with some rudimentary education. Ambedkar's grandfather was one of these recruits and his son, Ambedkar's father, became a teacher and eventually headmaster of an army school for Untouchables with the rank of "subhedar-major." It was from this raised threshold that Ambedkar had gotten his start. The English Protestant missionaries who began work in India at the end of the eighteenth century at first followed the earlier Catholic pattern of accommodating to the requirements of caste among their converts. Most of the early new Christians came from among the Untouchables and there was a strong desire among many to attract higher caste Hindus to the new faith. This led to an "Orientalist" view among some missionaries which held that the cultural patterns of the people should be left undisturbed. Others hotly contested any compromise between Christianity and caste and this led to long struggles between pastors and their flocks. There is a dramatic glimpse in one account of a doughty early missionary named Dr. John melting into one the two cups used separately for communion by the caste Christians and the Untouchables in his congregation.[17] That happened before 1812 and over the years that followed the issue continued to bedevil the church in India. Mission institutions did open up educational opportunities to Untouchables but this was done to a considerable extent by opening separate schools for their benefit. The British government also took an early stand against Brahmin resistance to non-Brahmin education and barred any discrimination or separation by caste in government-supported schools. In 1858 this principle was explicitly affirmed as applying to Untouchables. Although over the

17 "The Christians ... contended for distinct places at church and even for two cups at the Lord's Supper for the higher and lower castes. The latter ... were compelled to sit apart from the rest and to have their separate cup. At last Dr. John resolved to endure this anti-Christian custom no longer and gave notice that if they would not, of their own accord, put an end to these odious distinctions, especially at the Lord's table, he would himself abolish them. His admonitions being obstinately resisted, he executed his threat, with regard to the sacrament at least, by melting the two cups into one. This effectually settled the matter. The men of caste made a great outcry at first and left the church; but finding they could not intimidate their faithful pastor into a compliance with their wishes, they gradually returned, and henceforth drank out of one and the same cup with the Pariahs."—Quoted from James Hough, *The History of Christianity in India*, London, 1839, IV:203, by M. A. Sherring, *History of Protestant Missions in India 1706–1882*, London 1884, p. 349.

many decades the caste resistance in India "often produced more discretion than zeal in the enforcement of this rule," [18] the official attitude did represent a source of constant pressure on caste Hindus and did open opportunities for schooling to Untouchables. The impact of Western humanitarian, liberal, and rationalist ideas stirred several new Hindu reform movements beginning about the middle of the 19th century. One such reformer was Jyotirao Phule of Poona who began to advocate the very un-Hindu idea of "asserting the worth of man irrespective of caste." [19] Phule challenged the Brahmins first by opening a school for non-Brahmins in Poona in 1848 and three years later established what one account flatly calls "the first school in India for Untouchables." [20]

These assorted influences and activities came to bear in various ways and often in competition with each other during the following decades. Hindu reformers wanted in part to offset both Christian and Muslim counterinfluence among the lowlier Hindus. The British were involved in a complicated set of changing relationships with both Muslims and Hindus after the Sepoy Mutiny of 1857. There was also a burgeoning of self-assertion among the non-Brahmin Hindu castes against Brahmin domination. Out of all this came more chances for the lowly to go to school and to rise and some of these chances began to go to a few even among the Untouchables. Several Indian princes, notably in Baroda, Mysore, and Travancore, developed a philanthropic and political interest in this matter, both under the impetus of Hindu reformism and of their British advisers. The Maharajah of Baroda established a school for Untouchables in 1883 and it was on one of his scholarships that Ambedkar went to Columbia University in New York in 1913. Thereafter the process quickened, the

[18] Arthur Mayhew, *The Education of India, Study of British Educational Policy in India*, 1835–1920, London 1926, p. 259.

[19] Ghurye, *Caste and Race*, p. 165.

[20] Keer, p. 4, Ghurye, p. 166.

spur coming from several different directions. The first
World War had brought on increased nationalist pressure
in India and significant reforms were granted by the British
in the constitution of 1919, involving the grant of representation to various groups in India through separate electorates and the grant for the first time of some political representation (through nomination to various bodies) to the
"Depressed Classes," including the Untouchables. British
interest in the lowlier Hindus and in the Muslim and
Christian minorities became livelier as Hindu nationalist
pressure grew with the advent of Gandhi. Partly because he
was a reformer himself and also because he was a politician
interested in mass mobilization, Gandhi began to press caste
Hindus to see to reforms in their own system, to begin amend-
ing some of their practices, and particularly to do something
about improving the lot of the Untouchables. During this
same time, finally, the mid-1920's, Ambedkar appeared on
the scene, the first major leader to appear from among the
Untouchables themselves. Although his movement was largely
confined to his own group, the Mahars of Maharashtra, his
influence spread, his pressure and great personal force soon
winning recognition and some concessions to the demands
he made for Untouchables in general. Everybody was spurred
to some greater effort, especially in the educational field—
the British authorities, the missionaries, caste Hindu reformers and caste Hindu politicians. In this way from the
first few drops of the succor of learning that fell among the
parched Untouchables in the last years of the last century
came the beginnings of a trickle of educational opportunities
and this trickle began to widen into a small stream. Out of it
came a first generation of emergent educated Untouchables,
the first teachers, the first to take the few places opened to
them in government service, especially in some of the princely
states, the first to take place—whether under Ambedkar, or

more widely, under Gandhi—in the developing politics of the country. In the 1930's and 1940's, as more and more Untouchable children followed their paths into schools, these elders, still only a handful of individuals, took their part in the political struggle, the Congress movement, Gandhi's campaigns against the British, the war, the bloody Hindu-Muslim upheavals and collisions, and the coming of independence.

Until well into the 1930's, it plainly took some special circumstance or special person to bring an Untouchable child to school and to keep him there. As I met some of these individuals and began to listen to their stories of how they had gotten started, I became aware that this special person was very often a father, and the special circumstances some impulse, some drive, that had moved him to defy fate by sending his son to school. Some of these fathers were men who had gotten started themselves on the road to education —indeed, in general the rule seems to hold that the higher-achieving the sons, the better educated the fathers. But others were quite illiterate and yet had been moved in some way to put a son's small foot on the path that led to complete rejection of the fate which for so many centuries had been accepted without question. These fathers played their parts in this story of human change and, dimly as they may appear in this misty gallery, they are not to be passed by.

Around the turn of the century thousands of laborers used to go each year from the east coast of India for spells of work on the docks at Rangoon in Burma. One of these migrant laborers, a member of the Untouchable Mala caste of cowherds from an Andhra village, decided not to return with the others when their contract was up but to stay in Rangoon, where he managed to get himself apprenticed to a tailor and to learn this new trade. "He decided to change things, and to become another kind of man," his son told me. "He wanted me to be like him and not like all the others who went just to labor and come back. So he took me to Rangoon the year I was seven and for some years I learned how to be a tailor." In Rangoon the son went to school, later returned to India to go to high school and then on to the university and a career in politics inspired by Gandhi in the early 1920's. This was the story of the father of B. S. Murthy, a self-assured man now close to sixty, who became Deputy Minister of Community Development in the Nehru cabinet.

B. N. Kureel, who is forty-three and occupies a Congress Party seat in the Lok Sabha, or lower house of Parliament, from Uttar Pradesh, came of a family that was entirely illiterate. Kureel was the first in his family ever to go to school and when I asked him why his father had sent him, he said:

I wondered about this and only a few years ago I asked him. He is still there in the village, about eighty years old now. He told me that at that time he was feeling harassed by the zamindars [landlords] who were pressing the men of the village, including my father, for forced labor for them. One day, he said, it suddenly came to his mind: "If a son of my family were educated, this might not happen. It would never happen to *him*. So I decided to send you to school." That's what he said, and I went to school in a village a mile away.

B. P. Maurya, a Republican Party Member of Parliament, a Chamar from Uttar Pradesh, was also the son of a farm laborer, but his father was a man who had received the beginnings of an education. This came about because one day when he was a youth—it was back in the 1890's—an English Roman Catholic priest came to his village and offered to teach reading and writing to anyone who came. Three young

Chamars, of all in the village, went to him, all three of them, Maurya said, from the families that were relatively the best off among the Untouchables of the place. He learned to read and write a little Hindi in the time that the priest came. Maurya went on:

My father had strong feelings about education. "Only education will solve our problem," he would say. This is what he learned from that padre and he used to say it to us all the time. He used to say Untouchability would vanish when all people got educated. In his day Untouchables were treated like animals, and this is much changed now. He did not embrace Christianity with the padre and he did not embrace Buddhism although he followed Ambedkar in politics. He is still a Scheduled Caste Hindu. He is eighty-eight years old, and what he wants is to cease being a victim of Untouchability.

The story of a man who at forty is an M.A., and a Lecturer in History, presented a three-generation pattern with some rather special features. In his case, the early impetus came not from his father but from his grandfather, who quit the village early, went to work on the railroad and rose to be a fireman. "So long as my grandfather was there," he said, "we were in a good position." His father, however, took off on his own way, possibly getting some pleasure or satisfaction out of it but hardly becoming much of a help or spur to his son.

My father grew up a jolly person with an aptitude for singing. So long as my grandfather was there it was all right. I was the only child because my mother died when I was seven months old. My grandmother looked after me. The family was in Bombay and I went to primary school here. My father became a kind of wandering singer or poet, a composer of *lawani*, or songs in praise of old warriors. Such people were called *tamasgir*, or entertainers of soldiers in old times. A *tamasgir* is one who follows the profession of *tamasha*, being part of an entertainer group consist-

ing of a dancer, a comic, somebody who could play a noble
person, and a singer; and they also could all play instruments.
They would wander from place to place, making up songs, enter-
taining, singing ballads.

We have *tamasha* of various castes, Brahmin *tamasha*, Maratha
tamasha. My father learned *tamasha* at the feet of a Brahmin.
He never worked except at his singing profession which did not
pay very well. He didn't really earn anything. It is really a
begging profession, well, maybe not exactly begging, but having
to depend on whatever the public might feel like giving. The
money my father spent was earned by my grandfather. My father
wanted me to follow his profession of *tamasha*. But I went to
school without support from my father. I got a freeship as a
Scheduled Caste person and worked as a teacher when I was in
high school, teaching first and second standard,[21] for which I got
five rupees a month. This was in the British time. I passed my
matric in 1940.

There is a glimpse of another father who had come to the
city and found work as a laborer. Turning to one of the universal solaces of the frustrated poor, he nourished some deeply
glimmering impulses of his own. His son told me:

My father's pleasures were to drink wine and to have us read to
him from two books of the Mahabarata. He used to come home
in a drinking condition and ask us to read to him from these
books. This was when he would love his children most, when he
would come home after drinking at the wineshop and ask us to
read or sing. That is the way his day would finish—work, wine,
home, and work again. That was his life.

21 "Standards" in India are equivalent to American "grades." Secondary
schooling ends with the eleventh standard, one year sooner than in the American system. The usual arrangement provides for four years in primary school,
three in middle school, and four in high school. The successful matriculate or
"matric" may go to higher education, four years for a bachelor's degree in
arts (sometimes divided between a "pre-university" year and a three-year
degree course), or five years for a degree in science or technology.

From some of the younger men, we begin to discover fathers who had some slightly greater chance to change their lives if they would reach out to do so, and perhaps the most striking story of this kind came from a cool and self-confident man of thirty whose name is Sonavane and who is one of the small number of ex-Untouchables to pass the Class 1 civil service examination. He told me this story about his father:

My father's father died when he was only seven years old and my father worked as a laborer in the field. Another young man of the village, a relative of my father's, got an education with the help of the Maharajah of Kholapur. My father decided that he too would get an education. He was twenty-three years old when he made this decision. I was already in school, in the second standard at that time. People laughed at him, but he had determination in his mind and he was not deterred. The principal of the school helped him, and he did 11 years' work in four years, moving from vernacular first grade to matric (matriculation) which he passed in 1943. He now works in the Central Excise in Bombay, a Class 3 post, and he earns R429 a month.

In the accounts of men in their thirties and down into the twenties, we come on fathers who are still laboring in the villages, but by now they are often men who had one or two grades of primary school in the vernacular and this was often true of the mothers as well. We also begin to come on fathers who migrated at some point to the city and, in some cases, moved out of their traditionally menial occupations into some new and better kind of work. A Siddharth graduate who took a degree in chemistry and now works in the government meteorological service was the son of a man who came to Bombay as a youth and became a motor mechanic, and a mother who went as far as the 7th standard vernacular. Another rising young academic told me how his father came to the city from their Gujerat village and became a sign painter, eventually setting up a little sign-painting business of his own. The Registrar of the Siddharth College of Commerce is the son of a Mahar who was a Grade C fireman on the railway, worked all his life to put his eight children through school, and at fifty "began to read a little himself." A lecturer in mathematics at Siddharth is the grandson of a well-digger and the son of a man who learned to read and write from some Catholic priests who came to their village. This father went on to primary school and became a teacher, and has lived to see his sons win university degrees. Of the youngest under-graduates I met, around twenty years old, almost all had started from some slightly raised parental threshold. Several had parents who had finished primary school and become teachers. One father had become an inspector in the telephone company; another a truck driver in the same company; and a third had gone up to matriculation and become an employee in a large department store.

As some of these stories have shown, the initial impetus, usually from a father, also came sometimes from others in this gallery of men—the occasional foreign Christians who came with the offer of literacy, and more often, the caste Hindu teachers who accepted Untouchable children with a kind, helping spirit, and did what they could to move them along to some chance of a better life. Indeed, like so many other unique particulars in Indian life, even this impulse to help Un-touchables was, in a few of the cases mentioned, the product of tradition, in this case the particular tradition of a Kshatriya caste called "CKP" (Chandraseniya Kayastha Prabhu). This group, described as an intellectual community, came into con-flict with the Brahmins at least 300 years ago over their right to be teachers and scholars. As an act of special defiance of the Brahmins, CKPs of that distant day began helping Untouchables and as a consequence, as one ex-Untouchable told me, "they have had a soft feeling for Untouchables ever since." For this man it had been a CKP school principal who had given him his main chance to advance in school.

It not only took some rather special impetus to put these individuals on the road to an education, but it also took a special kind of persistence and courage to stay on this road. The lonely little boys who made their way to schools in many scattered places in India during the first 30 years of this century had to accept the bluntest kind of rejection and exclusion and had to be able to persist in the face of it year after year to get through. They could go *to* school, for example, but very rarely could they go *in*. Despite long-standing official policies of nondiscrimination, the Untouchable child almost invariably was made to sit outside in the dirt near the door or under a window, sometimes on the verandah if there was one, and take his lessons by listening from there. Where they were allowed to enter the classroom, they had to sit on separate benches or on the floor. Since so many of these individuals were "firsts" in their village or district, they usually sat out there in the dirt or apart in the classroom quite alone. One or two went to Christian mission schools set up especially for Untouchables and therefore did not have to face the problem of contact with caste Hindus until they reached the 5th standard in middle school. Some Christian schools, especially in the south where they were attended by caste Hindu children, also maintained some form of separation for the rare Untouchable child who came. Since schools were often quite a distance from home, it was frequently not only a matter of suffering exclusion from the classroom but also of finding a place to board. Untouchables would not be allowed to stay at school hostels or special arrangements had to be made for them to eat and sleep apart. Here is a typical account:

When I came to the school to which my father sent me, I was the first boy ever to come there from the Scheduled Castes. I had to sit separate, out on the verandah, and listen from the outside, and that is where I sat every day for three years. In the third year one day an inspector of schools came and put questions to the class and found me to be the best. He asked me why I was sitting outside. The teacher answered for me and said I belonged to the Chamars, that I was Untouchable, that the other boys wouldn't touch me. The inspector said that according to government rules, Untouchability could not be observed to such an extent and that some other arrangement would have to be made. So the teacher had me come inside and sit in a chair behind his chair, and that is where I spent the whole fourth year, sitting behind the teacher, facing the entire class. That was in 1928.

At age ten he was sent to a middle school, nine miles from his home. At the school hostel three boys ordinarily shared a room, but no one would share with him although the teacher in charge, "a kindhearted Brahmin, a Gandhian who wore khadi [homespun], tried to persuade the other boys," but failed. The problem was solved for a time by bringing in two other Untouchable boys whom the teacher agreed to take although they were at a much lower level.

An older man who went to school in Travancore early in the 1920's remembered:

I was able to go inside, although to sit on a separate seat. I was the only Scheduled Caste boy in the class and I had a seat in the corner. The teacher would not come near me. I would write on my slate and put it on the floor and he would come and look at it. Sometimes he would beat me and would do this by throwing his cane against my outstretched hand. It would hit my hand and then fall to the floor and he would pick it up and throw it again against my hand. He was an old man. I met him years later and reminded him how he beat me. He only smiled.

What made this example notable was that the school where it happened was a Catholic school, located in what is now the state of Kerala. In the south, Christians had for many generations simply continued the customary caste practices, with ex-caste Hindu Christians excluding ex-Untouchable Christians just as though nothing else had changed. This practice, long common among Catholics,[22] was also common among Anglicans of more recent date. The fact that the boy in this case had been allowed to enter the classroom at all was a recent and quite radical innovation at the time he attended, part of the post-1919 reforms encouraged by the Maharajah of Travancore. "This was better," he explained, "than in communities where the Nairs [a local upper caste group] were in control because they previously would not allow Untouchables to go to school at all, whereas the Christians allowed us to come and stand outside and, by the time I went, to come inside."

By the 1920's, signs of change multiplied. There were scholarships (maintenance stipends) being offered in some states for Untouchable children going to school, and various central government programs also offered help and encouragement. In Uttar Pradesh a lad of ten received six rupees a month to keep himself at a middle school. It was still early in the decade and he still prepared his food all by himself each day and sat outside in the dirt at the school. But a new era began one day when a new teacher appeared.

I was in the 5th standard when he came along and asked me why I was sitting outside. When I explained, he said: "Never mind, come in and sit on the bench." The other boys objected. Each bench was for six boys but they would not sit with me. They crowded onto other benches and I had a bench all to myself. That teacher was a Shudra (i.e., of low but touchable caste) and was quite bold. He wanted to eradicate these evils, he said, and he

22 Sanctioned by a special papal bull issued by Pope Gregory XV, says Ghurye, quoting the *Encyclopaedia Britannica*, 11th ed., V:468.

told the other boys: "If you don't want to sit here, you can leave."
By the next year in the 7th standard we were all sitting together.

In the last prewar years, there was rapid expansion of school
facilities, partly under the impetus of the new Congress
governments in the states, popularly elected for the first time
in 1937. This brought correspondingly broader opportunity
for Untouchables, especially in the cities. But it still called for
a strong drive and grim persistence for a youngster to make
his way ahead.

At high school I was a good student. I read my books under the
street lamps at night. The principal gave me a place to study in
the school building. The school was two miles from where I
lived. After school I would walk home and take food and then go
back to school to study for as long as I could. Then I would sleep
there on the floor. Early in the morning I went back home to eat
and then came back to school in time for the first class. There
were three or four of us doing this.

Great events heralded greater changes. The onset of war in
Europe and then in Asia itself brought on a major political
crisis in India. The quickening of the coming of change was
felt at every level of life. The youngest of the ex-Untouchable
undergraduates who told me about their fathers were born in
1940 or 1941, and were just about at school-starting age themselves in 1947 when the government of newly independent
India proclaimed the goal of free primary education for all.

5. THE SONS: EXPANDING EDUCATION

The sweep of millions of children into schools is one of the
great new facts of life in all the "new" countries. The sight
of them on the streets and roads is one of the new sights everywhere in Asia for anyone who remembers how thin the lines
of schoolchildren were only some 30 years ago. In India, the
closing years of British rule had seen great spurts in popular
education. After 1947, the channel was spectacularly widened
and deepened. In 1946–47, the year before independence, the
country's school population stood at 18,200,000 and the literacy
rate at about 10 percent. The school population now stands
at about 50,000,000 and the literacy rate is nearing 25 percent.
The number of schools of all kinds rose from 218,000 in 1946–
47 to 460,000 in 1961. A still largely illiterate generation of
parents is being divided more and more from the children
of these years by the widening gulf of education. The effects
of this change among such great masses of people are largely
incalculable and unforeseeable; it is probably the most important and most fateful of all the changes taking place among
people in our time.

In all of this the ex-Untouchables have shared in steeply
rising proportions. Precise figures about this are quite impossible to come by. Although the Indian government and
Indian states have spent millions of dollars to open special
educational opportunities to the former Untouchables, no one
has monitored the showing, a failure much too marked to be
seen merely as ignorance or the slipshod ways of bureaucrats,

or even as a task too great for the limited resources of a
society faced with so many vaster problems. It may be that the
legal act of abolition and the launching of these special programs of assistance allowed liberal-minded caste Hindus to
feel that they had "faced" the unpleasant fact of Untouchability. They did not want to look any harder or closer at what
was happening or at the people to whom it was happening.
(When I told a prominent educator and intellectual, an old
acquaintance, what I was trying to learn, he looked at me in
long silence and finally said: "How little imagination we
Indian intellectuals have! Here we are putting out crores
[tens of millions] of rupees on these programs for the Harijans
and nobody, nobody at all, seems to ask what this is as a
human problem, what does it mean to these people, nobody,
until someone comes from the outside and asks these questions!")

It took much patient inquiry and some hard digging by
embarrassed but obliging officials at the Home and Education ministries in New Delhi to get even a few clues from
which some guesses might be made about some of the larger
statistics. Part of the difficulty arose because one of the ways
the Indian regime has shadow-boxed against caste has been to
eliminate listing by caste in government record-keeping, a
blow which left no mark on the caste system but has made it
aggravatingly more difficult for anyone to discover in any
precise way what has been happening in the society in this
respect. From the figures I did get, however, it seems possible
to estimate that in 1948–49 there were well over half a million
Untouchables in Indian schools. In 15 years, while the total
school population has more than doubled, the figure for
ex-Untouchables has swelled eightfold or tenfold to some
6,000,000, including more than 4,000,000 ex-Untouchable
children in primary schools (which are now largely free to
all), something close to 1,500,000 in middle and high schools

(in which the Scheduled Castes are exempt from fees and in many places receive supporting stipends), and about 55,000 in colleges and universities and various other technical and other higher schools. The last is nearly a hard figure: in 1963 the government of India gave 55,568 scholarships to ex-Untouchables in higher education.

But once we got this far among the large items, no one could even guess at figures to suggest how things were going, especially at the higher levels of education. There are thousands of Scheduled Caste teachers now, but no one knows how many. The annual grant of central government scholarships reached the figure given, 55,568, in 1963, and the annual totals added each year since the program began (in the British time, in 1944–45, with the grant of 114 scholarships) produce a grand total of 307,187 individual annual scholarships given, at a total outlay of R129,570,000, or about $27,200,000 at current exchange. But no one knows how many bodies this total represents. No one knows how many dropped by the wayside, how many finished. India turns out 140,000 graduates at the bachelor's degree level each year. If a guess by one of my top official informants is correct, 2 percent, or about 2,800 of these are ex-Untouchables. Of those who have won degrees, no one knows how many have won "firsts," how many received "second class" degrees, and how many pass-class. The truth is that in any broad statistical way, nobody knows anything about this at all. "We don't have performance figures from the schools," the Deputy Commissioner for Scheduled Castes and Tribes told me. A diligent assistant who combed the files at my request came up with the news that a circular had gone out to the state governments in 1961 asking for this kind of information but no replies had ever come in. There were only fragments to guess on. The most substantial information of this kind I subsequently received was a set of figures prepared for the Planning Commission showing that in July, 1963, there were 307,133 members of the Scheduled Castes on the live registers of the Employment Exchanges, of whom some two-thirds had less than an eighth grade education, 43,328 were matriculates, and 2,362 university graduates. Of these latter groups, about three-quarters had achieved third class standing in their final examinations, a quarter second class, and only 822 individuals, or 1.8 percent, first class. No comparative figures were given, but it was inferred that the ex-Untouchable showing was markedly poorer than that of caste Hindus on these lists. The figures do show, however, how educated ex-Untouchables are adding to the swollen totals of educated unemployed in India, given here for July, 1963, as 709,546 unemployed "matrics" and 69,959 unemployed graduates.

At the Ministry of Education, another official produced an interesting fragment about the 1962 competition for 13 Government of India overseas scholarships, a rich plum for which all applicants had to hold first-class degrees. In a field of several hundred applicants, 72 were members of Scheduled Caste, and five of them were awarded scholarships. The vital ingredient here is the indication that there were at least 72 first-class degree holders who were ex-Untouchables, a quite respectable number. Other fragments turned up elsewhere. In the south, at the University of Mysore, which has 40,000 students in some 60-odd colleges around the state, I was told there were 961 ex-Untouchables in the entering class. This is the so-called "pre-university course," the last hurdle students must get over in order to enter upon the three-year degree course. At Mysore only 30 percent of all pre-university hopefuls get through into the degree course. Among the Scheduled Caste students in this group, less than 6 percent get through. One school had figures to show that 70 out of every 100

Brahmin students pass while only 5 out of every 100 ex-Untouchables do so. At the University of Bombay, a young man in the registrar's office went to considerable work to assemble for me figures that showed that in 1961–62, 328 Scheduled Caste students presented themselves to be examined at the end of first year Arts, and that of these only 88 passed and were able to go on to the second year, called "intermediate" or "inter-arts." In the second year group, 348 appeared for examination—and there was no way of knowing how long these students had taken to reach this point or how many times they had taken the examination before—and of these only 27 passed. In the degree year, 73 ex-Untouchables appeared, and of these 33 passed and were awarded degrees. As far as the available figures seemed to indicate, this appeared to be about half as good as the performance of caste Hindu students at the university.

In Siddharth College, operated by the People's Education Society, founded by Ambedkar in 1946, there are now some 2,500 students in the arts college, of whom 600 are of the Scheduled Castes. There are also associated commerce and law schools with smaller numbers and smaller percentages of ex-Untouchables. Ex-Untouchables come to this school in greater numbers than they go elsewhere mainly because Siddharth is in a way "theirs" and they feel more "at home" here, but also because it admits them down to a score of 35 percent on their matriculation examinations, compared to an admitting floor of 70 percent or better in many other institutions. Although Siddharth is so much more hospitable in its admission policy, its students must take the same university examinations and the going is tough. Principal H. R. Karnik, a caste Hindu educator who headed Siddharth Arts and Sciences for about eight years, told me that of 300 ex-Untouchables admitted each year in Arts, about 60 make it into the second year, and that of these 15 or 16 go on to finish. In Science, which is much more demanding—they have to maintain a schedule which prevents them from working at outside jobs—only 50 or 60 will enter in a given year and of these 8 or 10 will eventually win degrees by going on from Siddarth to other more advanced schools of science and technology. Given their backgrounds and the conditions in which they have to work as students, Principal Karnik thinks this is a showing to be respected. He said:

About half of our Scheduled Caste students are from the local Bombay population and the rest from rural areas outside. The city students are the sons of laborers. Most of their fathers are uneducated, most of them illiterate. There are hardly any exceptions to this. Mahars could go to free public schools here beginning about 25 years ago. They used to sit in corners, but Ambedkar got that abolished. Consciousness of education among the Mahars was created by the Ambedkar movement. He urged them to get educated, to get their children educated. In Bombay province, the Scheduled Castes began to go to primary school around 1935. All our students went to free schools in the villages or in Bombay. Their chance for higher education did not come really until Ambedkar established the People's Education Society and founded these schools in 1946 and then, after 1947, when the government scholarship program was expanded after independence. All our students are here on government scholarships, which pay them 25 rupees [$5.25] a month and are exempt from fees which run to 300 rupees [$63] a year for Arts and 380 rupees [$80] for Science. If they stay in our hostel, their mess fee is paid, 27 rupees [$5.70] a month. In Arts they are free at noon and some get jobs and earn more than their scholarship pays them. In that case they remain exempt from fees but do not get the scholarship. I'd say more than half of the 600 are working this way, all at low grade jobs that pay them perhaps 120 rupees [$25] a month. There are 200 students in Science, taking physics, chemistry, biology, and mathematics. That course runs to 4:30 P.M., and they cannot work outside. On the Arts side they take humanities and social sciences. These two courses are completely separate. Arts leads to clerical jobs. Science leads to the chance to go to technological institutions and better jobs, such as chemists. Our first graduates, about a dozen, came out in 1950. I have been here eight years and since that time we have had four, maybe five, first class degrees. One of our students made it into I.A.S. [Indian Administrative Services, the Class 1 civil service] from the general list, the others with the help of the reservations. We have four Scheduled Caste lecturers, three of them graduates of Siddarth. You need a 2nd class degree to be hired and very few have so far gone for postgraduate courses here, and very few of these achieve the 2nd class M.A. We have four Scheduled Caste lecturers out of a staff of 25, and 14 tutors out of 38. I am not happy about these showings, but it is not their fault that very few of them are good students. It is because of the conditions under which they have to work. They live in places where the whole family lives in one room, eight or ten people. Students simply cannot study. Our hostel can accommodate only 100 Scheduled Caste students, and this means that over 500 have to stay at their homes. How is a student going to manage if he does not have a chance to read a book where he lives, no table, no chair, no light? Most of them read in the library here, which is open until 10 o'clock.

The Registrar of Siddharth College of Commerce, a heavy-set young man of twenty-seven whose name is Ubale and who holds M.A. and LL.B. degrees, insisted that we had to see for ourselves how educated ex-Untouchables live in Bombay, so we fixed a time to visit him at his home. He came to our hotel to get us and we took a taxi for what proved to be a long ride across a good stretch of the city of Bombay. We pulled swiftly away from Marine Drive and the downtown neighborhoods where the new Indian middle class is filling comfortable-looking, even luxurious new apartment blocks, out through streets lined with their parked cars, out past quarter after quarter of more modest middle-class, working-class, and slum Bombay, through miles of suffocatingly crowded streets choked with traffic and people. Next to a vast block of low-cost government tenements, we came to the edge of a great open hollow, a huge shallow craterlike space every square foot of which was covered by what first looked like a mass of debris but was actually a mass of human dwellings. We left the taxi at the road's edge outside and went on by foot, sometimes across planks laid across mud, sometimes in the mud. We picked our way along the narrow lanes between the rows of houses put together out of every conceivable kind of junk, wooden boxes, pieces of corrugated tin, old doors and windows, pieces of wallboard, roofs of thatch or tin or wood, all the ingenious improvisations of the universal squatter shackville, with little rivulets of sewage running down each alley or street, naked or half-naked children running about, and people in the various postures of the utmost kind of squalid poverty. The masses of shacks were clustered in and around an occasional more substantial building, long, narrow, and high, with walls of brick and roofs of tin or tile. These were the original barrack buildings of Rawaly Camp, once an establishment for British troops at the city's edge, and the place was still known by that name. These barrack buildings had been partitioned off into rooms of approximately 10 by 18 feet. In each of these a family lived. I have to confess that I thought Ubale had taken us into Rawaly Camp to show us how the lowest of the low live before taking us elsewhere to his own place, but he led us now into one of these ex-barracks rooms which turned out to be his own family's home.

Ubale's room was swept bright and clean. His young wife and two small children, a brother-in-law and his wife, waited there to greet us. Most of the people in Rawaly Camp got water from taps spaced at long intervals out in the lanes, but

Ubale had piped water into his room and had brought an electric line over from the nearest building in the tenement block nearby. Several of the rooms in the barracks had these amenities, making theirs the best housing in the area. The Ubale room was divided by a semi-partition made up of a cabinet which held household supplies. On a shelf over the water tap a little row of brass pots and bowls gleamed in the half-dark at the end of the room. A low single kerosene burner on the floor provided heat for cooking. Near the front of the room was a low table and small benches. At night, Ubale explained, they pushed these aside, spread some mats, and slept on the floor. On a shelf near the door stood some of Ubale's books and some family pictures. The bare electric bulb hung from a cord over our heads. Smiling her bashful smile, Mrs. Ubale laid cups of tea and bowls of sweetened noodles before us while we talked and learned something about the economics of the Ubale household. For this room Ubale paid 23 rupees, or not quite $5 a month. Food cost 100 rupees ($21), clothing 10 rupees ($2.10) and medical costs were usually 15 rupees ($3.15.) His salary at Siddarth is R300 ($63) and he would just about be able to manage on this except that he is paying R100 a month on a loan of R2,000 ($420) he contracted for his sister's marriage the year before. His last sister was about to be married and he had borrowed another R2,000 to launch her properly. It would cost him R100 a month for the next four years to pay off these debts. It was impossible in any case to move now to some better locality because of the high cost of *pagdi*, the illegal premium that we would call "key money" which is needed to rent any space at all. For this room when he took it the year he married, in 1958, Ubale had paid R1,000 ($210) simply to move in. This has to be paid to the previous holder of the lease. "To move out of here now, I could not take less than

R4,000 ($840)," he explained, "because in any better locality I would have to pay at least R5,000 ($1,050) to the occupants or to the landlord. I will have to borrow to make up any difference. If I find I cannot move to a better area, I will have to look for a larger place in another slum area." I ventured to wonder out loud why, in view of these facts and figures, it wasn't possible to spend something less than half a year's salary on a wedding, especially since the money had to be borrowed, and this young man, who was moving in a stream flowing against the ancient Law of Manu and 2,000 years of Hindu tradition, replied: "Oh, you can't go against custom, otherwise our own people would look down on us! We spend R2,000 on a wedding here and we wouldn't spend less than R1,000 even in the village. About 700 or 800 people will come. We hire a hall for the occasion. My sister," he added proudly, "appeared for the Secondary School Certificate and she is marrying a B.A."

Ubale waved at the squalid heaps and shacks outside and said there were 4 B.A.s and LL.B.s living in Rawaly, probably about 50 successful matriculates, and as many as 1,000 young men working toward the matric exam. They were living out in those shacks many of which, he said, were also so-called "black spots" or places where illegal liquor was made and sold, a major slum occupation. About 25,000 people live in Rawaly Camp, and other localities like it dot the city, many larger or smaller shackvilles occupying hollows or other low places in and around the slums of the city. There are between 500,000 and 700,000 ex-Untouchables in Bombay—no one was sure of that figure either—and the bulk of them live in places like Rawaly Camp. We walked out back along the narrow lanes. The children, full of that particular vigor of the fittest who have survived, were racing around the place, only a few stopping to watch us go by. We reentered our cab and rode back through the great blocks of slums that now looked

positively luxurious, back into the upper-class neighborhoods that seemed to be located on another planet, and out
along the famous curving strand of Marine Drive where great
crowds of people were, as always, slowly strolling along the
sea's edge to feast their eyes on its open space and breathe in
some of its clean air.

6. MOVING UP

Through all the clogged shallows and over all the obstacles, a steadily rising number of educated ex-Untouchables is making its way to new levels in the Indian society. There are hundreds of thousands of them moving up and they are being pushed by millions of youngsters coming up behind them in the primary and secondary schools. They are coming up, moreover, alongside millions of other young Indians who are caste Hindus but who also were never part of an educated class in India before. One can only guess at how they will relate to each other and what their future roles will be in a changing Indian society. Much might be said about the kind of education they are getting, and the kind of educated people they are becoming, and much also, in the face of all the "planning," about the blindness of the process of change. The shape of the future depends on the pace and manner of India's conquest of its backwardness and this in turn depends, in part only but heavily, on what happens elsewhere in the world. These remain imponderables and meanwhile these masses of young people keep coming out of the schools to add more grievous numbers each year to India's already grievous problem of educated underemployed or unemployed; no one knows for sure how many they are but everyone knows they are growing more numerous every year. The ex-Untouchables, coming from so much farther down, have to struggle all the harder to come up, or at least have a longer way to rise. All the entrenched sanctions and habits of the Hindu caste system still stand in their way. The government, itself caught by so much ambivalence and conflict over the caste system, is committed to giving the ex-Untouchables special help. It is doing this not only by helping them through school but in opening the way afterward to jobs. Since ex-Untouchables cannot hope to find jobs in a society still dominated by caste-bound Hindus, the government has opened its own services and has set up quotas of reserved places for them to fill as they qualify. This system of "reserved places" or "reservations" began well back in the British time, mainly for the benefit of the non-Brahmin lower castes, and came partly as a result of the non-Brahmin fight against Brahmin domination. It has been enormously expanded by the government of independent India. It is now the lifeline by which more and more people are pulling themselves—or are being pulled—out of the cesspools of Untouchability.

Of the earlier generation of Untouchables who made their way upward through the educational opportunities opened up in the British time, some found places in politics, in Maharashtra through Ambedkar and his Scheduled Castes Federation, and many more elsewhere in India via the patronage of Gandhi and the Congress Party. In Gandhi's party—Gandhi was in this, as in all things, *bapu,* or father—the ex-Untouchables came to occupy a peculiarly favored position as wards, individuals selected for advancement, and as holders of seats reserved for them in the various legislatures at the center, in the states, and in the municipalities. Last year's president of the All-India Congress Party was an ex-Untouchable, an able younger politician named Sanjivaya who had risen to be Andhra's First Minister. Jagjivan Ram, a big, burly man with the easy-flowing speech of the practiced politician, served as Minister of Railways and then as Minister of Communications, leaving the cabinet after ten years as one of those affected by Nehru's shakeup of his regime late in 1963.

Sanjivaya, the first ex-Untouchable to serve as president of the Congress Party, entered the cabinet as Minister of Labor, thus keeping Scheduled Caste personalities in full view in top posts. B. S. Murthy, whose career also began with Gandhi in the 1920's, is Deputy Minister of Community Development, and Dr. M. M. Das is Deputy Minister of Science and Culture. Ex-Untouchables occupy 72 of the 495 seats in the House of the People in the central Parliament, and 477 seats among the 3,283 in the various state legislatures. Many of these seats are already occupied by younger arrivals on the political scene, products of the post-independence system of aided education and promotion by preferment.

No comparable visibility has been achieved by ex-Untouchables in the academic profession. "There are no Harijan intellectuals," flatly said one well-informed caste Hindu scholar and educator. "The older men who came up became politicians. A new group now coming up is moving into the universities, but they will be found still in fairly junior positions and almost all in the traditional branches of learning, not moving into fields where one might do research, for example, on the problems of the community. I would guess, however, that there may be as many as 100 Scheduled Caste Ph.D.s now, where ten years ago there were none." At the University of Mysore—where unusual opportunities opened earlier for the Scheduled Castes when it was a princely state— I was told there were ten ex-Untouchable Lecturers (equivalent to an American Assistant Professor) out of a total of one hundred, three Readers (equivalent to Associate Professor), one Professor, a dean of a medical college, and a college principal who holds a Ph.D. in botany. The University of Bombay, I learned, has produced two Ph.D.s in sociology and is about to produce a third, and ten M.A.s in this field since 1951. In this matter too, however, as in so many others, the numbers

get vague. There are instances in which ex-Untouchables who
attain faculty positions sometimes become less easily identi-
fiable. I met one high administrative officer at one university
who had been specifically named as an ex-Untouchable, but
he never so identified himself to me. There are some caste
Hindus who are glad to be able to make use of this occasional
fact. At the University of Delhi, for example, which had come
under some public criticism for failure to give adequate opportunities to members of the Scheduled Castes, one former
high officer of the institution told me he just could not say
whether there were any Scheduled Caste members in the
university's own faculty of 250 or among the 1,500 of the
staffs of its associated colleges. "A Harijan never likes to ad-
vertise the fact that he's a Harijan," he remarked rather de-
fensively. Farther down the line in the educational system
there are now great numbers of ex-Untouchable teachers,
many thousands of them, but, as we have already remarked,
no one knows just how many. Most of them are still humble
graduates themselves of little more than the primary grades
or secondary schools, but they are playing a key role in
widening the path up which they had traveled and along
which vastly greater numbers are following them.

In the world of business and professions there is still, by
all accounts, only the tiniest trickle of ex-Untouchables.
Employment in private business firms in India is still heavily
determined by regional, caste, and family connections. Mobility in this respect is only just beginning in the larger enterprises to cut across these lines. The chances are, I was told,
that the rare few ex-Untouchables who have moved successfully into business and commerce have managed in some way
to conceal their identities. This was the case in the two very
modest examples I myself ran into, one a man who was working for a trade association, and the other the father of a
student who had made his way to a white collar position in a

department store. As to other professions, I gathered only a few fragmentary indications. I asked staff members of several newspapers if there were any Scheduled Caste journalists and drew only blank stares of surprise at my question. There is apparently quite a scattering, however, of doctors and lawyers. In Bombay I was told that there are nine Scheduled Caste lawyers trying to practice privately but only one practicing physician, and that one a young woman whom I met, Dr. Shinde. She holds the degree the British call "Bachelor of Medicine and Bachelor of Surgery"—the M.B.B.S.—and has set up her own clinic in the city. In Madras, a caste Hindu journalist friend told me, "There are ten Harijan doctors who seem to be getting along all right." There are larger numbers who hold medical and law degrees and others qualified as engineers and chemists but they are all, I was usually told, working for the government.

At the lower occupational levels considerable change has come in the shift of great numbers of ex-Untouchables from village to city. Figures on this would probably show that relatively impressive numbers of former Untouchables have moved into industrial occupations, although large numbers have remained within the boundaries of their traditional occupations. Among those whose individual experiences I explored directly, the pattern of migration was a common one. The father, sometimes the grandfather, had come into the city from the village, and such people are in their many thousands the scavengers and sweepers who carry away the waste of India's great cities and who continue in their new situations, as we have already seen, many of the conditions and divisions they brought with them from their villages. Many others have gone to work in industry, though still as menials, as sweepers, as common laborers, dockworkers, stevedores, and the like. But many who have had some education, if only a few grades, have moved up, becoming truck and bus drivers, and workers on the railroads—where they moved into the slots vacated by many Anglo-Indians at the time of independence —and have begun rising through the grades of firemen on the way to becoming engine drivers. For those who are more enterprising and push up higher on the educational ladder, there is always the magic step up and out of manual labor altogether—the goal of goals for the aspiring Indian. Any manual labor in India is still held to be part of a low estate and it is the primary function of education, many still think, to emancipate them from it. In Bombay the law stipulates that no one who has passed the matriculation examination may be kept in a manual job. At the municipal transport yard where my Brahmin acquaintance showed me around and told me about his problems with Scheduled Caste drivers, he pointed out one young man in a white shirt tabulating records on a long white sheet. He had become a pretty good man on the motors, he told me, but he also went to school and when he passed the matric, they had to make him a clerk.

Following individuals on their way up, one pattern became familiar through its recurrence: the higher a father went, the higher a son could reach. The case of the Class 1 civil servant who was the son of a Class 3 civil servant was characteristic. In a group of youngsters I met in the south, there was one lad whose father works in a railway boiler shop who told me he wanted to become an engineer. Another was the son of a farmer who had managed to acquire a piece of land of his own; he wanted to become a doctor. The one ex-Untouchable I met in Bombay who is in private business is the son of a man who came to the city from the village and found a new kind of work in the railway paintshops. Quite a few high-aimers were the sons of men who had gone far enough in school themselves to have become teachers.

One also got from these individual family stories a quite literal sense of the swelling numbers of young people moving swiftly beyond their parents to higher and higher levels. Where the father had begun to move up, not one son but four or six moved higher, and so did his daughters. One student of law, who is the son of a tanner, has one brother who is a government clerk, another a factory inspector, and a younger brother now in his second year of science. The son of the department store employee has one brother with a Bachelor of Commerce degree who is now working in the government sales tax office, another brother who passed his matriculation and is working for the same firm as his father does, and two sisters moving up the school grades. The son of a primary school teacher has an older brother who holds a Master of Science degree and works for the government. Ubale, whose home we visited in Rawaly Camp, is the son of a Grade C fireman on the railway. Of his four brothers, one, a matric, now works for the railroad; another, a B.A., is in the government service; the third, who will appear for his B.A. this year, meanwhile has a job in a private insurance company. His youngest brother has taken a step beyond them all by entering not Siddarth but the University of Bombay.

But this rule too had its exception. Probably the most spectacular example of self-generated forward drive I came upon in this quest was that of Khadtale, the solidly chunky young man who had become a pilot for Indian Airlines. The son of a laborer who had never gone to school at all but whose children had, Khadtale made his way up to an engineering school in Poona along with 30 other Scheduled Caste boys. He failed several times, but kept trying. All his classmates of that time are now working for the government, he told me, with one exception who is working as an engineer in a private automobile concern where his employer does not know he is an ex-Untouchable. With his degree in science, Khadtale landed a job in the state aviation department and found himself working in the control tower at

the Bombay airport. Here he conceived the ambition to learn
to fly and with the help of government scholarships he did
so, winning his wings as pilot of a single-engine plane in
1955. From there he pushed on to commercial pilot training.
For this there were no scholarships, no reserved places—who
would ever have dreamed of an ex-Untouchable reaching
so far up? Khadtale hoarded his own money and talked
himself into loans and grants from a great variety of places
and ultimately from the Ministry of Social Welfare. After
several intervals when his money ran out, Khadtale finished
his training in 1959 and got his first job with a private
cargo plane company, Kallinga Airlines, flying old Dakotas
(the Douglas DC3) between points in India, the Middle
East and Africa; the son of an illiterate Untouchable laborer,
born and raised in the town of Nasig, was spanning the con-
tinents. In 1961 he was taken on by Indian Airlines as a
pilot, and a great astonished fuss was made in the newspapers
over this man who had come all the way up from the bottom
of the cesspool into the sky. Still flying co-pilot when we met,
Khadtale was expecting his own two-engine command mo-
mentarily and was looking ahead to a move to four-engine
aircraft and to jets.

Alongside this, one other example of high ambition sticks
in my mind. The elder son of a well-placed government
official had gone, like most educated ex-Untouchables, into
a safe government job after getting his college degree. But
the younger son was thinking of different things. When he
finished school, he said, he was going to go into business, and
what is more, he expected to do very well very fast. "I'm
going to be a millionaire," he said.

Upward-moving ex-Untouchable boys obviously have to
marry upward-moving ex-Untouchable girls. This is getting
easier to do now than it was, but it still presents problems.

Marriage out of caste is still quite rare and radical in all
parts of Indian society, and all the more so, of course, where
ex-Untouchables are concerned. In the beginning, only boys
moved out onto the path of education and it has only been
in more recent years, with the opening of public education
on a large scale, that girls have joined the general movement
across the great divide of literacy. Along this way, marriage
has been a problem, often an unhappy tangle. A common
Indian story of these years—and not only for the ex-Untouchable—is the story of the early marriage, made in the traditional
way, that cannot survive the changed life that comes with
education and the move out into the world. This happened
to many young ex-Untouchables, as a Chamar from Uttar
Pradesh told me:

Most of the boys are already married. These marriages might
have been made at age six, though the wives do not come to
join their husbands until they are sixteen. When the boys go to
school and grow up and the time approaches for them to fulfill
these marriages, it is then that they often seek a divorce. They
don't want to have illiterate wives. Their parents ask them to
accept these wives but many refuse at this time. This is a kind
of divorce, and the family has to pay a penalty because the
marriage is not fulfilled. Others do obey their parents and go on
with the ceremony and stay with their wives two or three years.
But this leads to troubled lives and they finally also often get
divorces. A penalty must be paid in this case to the panchayat
[caste council] when the girl leaves. She will try to marry someone else in some other place. In some cases it is the other way
around, the girls seeking the divorce, but this is very rare. If
there are children and the father wants them, he keeps them,
for this is the law, Hindu law and also government law. If the
mother does not want them, the father must keep them in any
case. This is also the law. I would guess that at least half of
the 48,000 who received scholarships this past year are married in
this manner.

But now it is becoming the custom not to marry early, because of this trouble with illiterate wives and because of the greater knowledge people have of the new opportunities. A new idea of change is going on in many villages where there is now compulsory education or where it is now more usual for everybody to go to school.

Girls are moving more and more into the channels of education and move up themselves to become teachers, nurses, and to higher education. This has been true longer for caste Hindu women, but ex-Untouchable girls are now getting their chance along with all the others. I met three such ex-Untouchable women, one of them who had earned a Ph.D. in England and had returned to the high post of Reader at her university; the practicing physician I have already mentioned; and the third, a bright young woman who was the only one of her sex among the competitors for Class 1 appointments at the coaching school I visited in Bangalore. Of the three only the physician was married. She was the daughter of an educated father but she married the son of a much humbler man of her community who had also risen through education and had become a practicing lawyer. She was the only one I met who spoke up in a more positive way about marriages across different educational levels. "It is true," she said, "there are not enough educated girls and some men sometimes have to marry uneducated girls. There are many families like this. That would be like my father and mother who are absolutely happy!"

In both the other cases there was some discouragement about the outlook for marriage. Ex-Untouchable men in India are no different from caste Hindu men or their similars in many other modernizing countries: they want their mates to be educated but not *too* educated and certainly not more educated than they are. This is something of a handicap for the girl who is gifted and ambitious. The young lady I met in Bangalore who had set her sights on a Class 1 government post had apparently brushed aside the question of marriage altogether. She was a light-skinned, well-dressed young woman who was quite aware of her unusual situation and rather pleased with it. She told me that the women of her village in northern Mysore had said to her: "You study, and then you don't get married, what's the use?" She had more directly personal reasons for not wanting to think of marriage—her own parents were separated—but she said she had heard that educated girls had unhappy marriages and she preferred to think of making her life in community service. "High officials often do not care for the people," she said. "I want to go into welfare activity, in education for women. My own caste people are ignorant and do not know the importance of education." The Class 1 civil service takes qualified women —five had made it in the country the previous year, she said— but the rule is that if a woman marries while in the service, she has to resign, with the option of dropping down to a Class 2 post. "In any case," she said, "it is difficult to find a boy of our level of education in our caste. I don't want to marry. I don't want to leave my mother, and men are not good, they don't give freedom and equality to women."

Quite a few of the young men I met had not been caught in early marriages arranged by their parents and they usually said they were waiting to get more settled in their lives before finding someone to marry. Among the Mahars, with their longer tradition of seeking education, there seemed to be no great problem now of finding educated girls. "There are many girl matriculates, even many graduates," I was told. In other caste groups the difficulty is greater but hardly insuperable. "I want an educated girl interested in social service," an Ada-Andhra boy told me in the south. "In my village there is no one I can marry. I will have to find one."

He happened to be a very handsomely dark young man, as so many are in south India, and I asked him whether color would figure in his choice. "In my community all are dark," he answered. "Maybe the Brahmins are not quite so [colored] —[not quite so "colorful" is what he actually said!]—but this is not a problem, this is not the way to distinguish people. In a girl I would prefer character and conduct and taste, no matter what color." He laughed a nervous little laugh then, and went on: "It is true that lighter girls will not prefer darker boys in any community. This is a matter of personal taste. If a man is dark, he has to be rich or educated. When parents arrange marriages, they compare complexions. It has to be what we call 'edo-jodu'—equal as the equal sign—in many things and color is one of the things. It is true that darker boys prefer lighter girls. If we are educated and wealthy, nobody will mind if we are dark. If you are poor, whether dark or light, people *will* mind, no doubt about that!"

There was usually no question at all about marrying inside the community. This was always assumed. For most of these young men the radical change was not an out-of-caste marriage, but choosing their own mates. "I will marry in my own community," said a Shangar boy in Mysore in a typical answer, "but *I* will choose the girl. There are few who are educated and I will have to find one of them somehow!" But in a few instances boys did raise their sights above the caste line. "If my father finds a girl for me," said the son of a politician, "it will be in our own community. If I find a girl for myself, it might be outside." Another young man thought intermarriage was the only way to solve the caste problem. "I want to marry outside," he said, "because it is the only way to abolish Untouchability. If you come together in marriage, you forget the past." The father of a growing son said to me somewhat musingly: "I want to choose a wife for my son and I might seek a wife outside our caste. This is not possible now in most cases, it's not likely, but I would like to." Then he added with vehemence: "I certainly will not choose a village girl for my son!"

A small drama of love across caste lines—a drama without words—turned up in a conversation with a small, rather pleasantly ugly young man (he reminded me somehow of Will Rogers, especially when he wrinkled his nose in smiling confusion, which was often) who told me first that he was not married and would not do anything about marriage until he was settled in a good government post. "It will be left to me to choose my own mate," he said, and smiling slyly, he continued: "And I desire to take a Brahmin girl, an Ayungar. I have the desire to marry her. She was in my class at college. No, I never spoke to her and she never spoke to me. I never got the courage to speak to her. She is not acquainted with me, but whenever I see her, I think she should be my wife, not because she is Brahmin, but because I feel something toward her." Is she beautiful, I asked, entranced. "Ah yes," he said. "She has attracted me—" and then hastily adding— "but it's not I that attracted her, she does not even know me! It is all my own desire, to marry her. Yes, I will ask her, I will definitely ask her as soon as the examination is over. I will ask her personally." I wondered whether he had any idea how she would reply. "No," he said, "I do not know what she will say. I don't know what she will say when I ask her. I have known her for four years and we have never spoken." "Did she ever show any interest at all in you?" I asked. "Oh, no," he said giggling nervously. "She's never shown interest in me. But I will ask her, I will definitely ask her!"

7. *JOBS BY RESERVATION:*
THE QUOTA SYSTEM

Almost all educated ex-Untouchables move into government jobs. This has been up to now the open channel and it has led several hundred thousand former Untouchables to new and better places in the society. These places have been reserved for them by explicit percentage quotas at every level of government employment. This system had its beginnings in India at least forty years ago coming as part of the revolt against Brahmin domination by the non-Brahmin castes, especially in the south. The reservation of government posts for non-Brahmins led to the opening of some places for Untouchables who qualified, especially in some of the princely states, and some of them rose rung by rung to fairly high places. In the state of Mysore there are now five or six district commissioners—senior administrative officers—who are members of Scheduled Castes. A small number of men of this generation have risen to senior posts in the central government services as well. Special benefits and reserved places for Untouchable and other groups were quite strongly established in the central and state governments in the closing decades of British rule. These were greatly enlarged after independence when the new Indian government set out to help raise the lowly by providing special channels of preferment both in education and in jobs.

This system of reservations was laid out for the benefit of

the Scheduled Castes, the aboriginal Scheduled Tribes, and a third huge omnibus category called "Other Backward Classes." In its first years, this program was challenged in the courts and the new Indian Constitution, at first based on the premise of recognition of equality of all citizens before the law, was duly amended to give the government power to practice some inequality in reverse in order to give these lower groups a chance to rise more rapidly. The provision for reserved seats in Parliament, originally set to last until 1960, was renewed and is likely to be renewed again, but no time limit was placed on other forms of special assurance. The Indians did not have much difficulty overcoming the contradiction between their very new formal official doctrine of equality and their effort to practice discrimination-in-reverse for the backward classes. This kind of contradiction was, after all, a familiar part of the traditional system, although it always usually worked in the opposite direction, against and not for the lowly. But they did run into a lot of trouble and great confusion over the matter of who in India was "backward." The criterion used was caste, the assumption being made that certain castes were by definition "backward." It quickly became clear, however, that the great bulk of India's multitude of castes considered themselves "backward" enough to be counted among the deserving poor and to share in any benefits that were being handed around. A government commission in 1953 named 2,399 such deserving castes and communities with an estimated total population of about 120,000,000. In many states a great clamor arose, with all kinds of groups insisting that they too should be classified as "backward" and these included, it must be said, some pretty forward castes who felt that their jealously guarded ritual or social superiority should not be allowed to interfere with their right to get on the government gravy train. One state tried to meet the problem by distinguishing between "backward" and "more backward" and another sorted out the "backward" from the "most backward." In the south these matters had long been wrapped up in the struggle of the lower castes against the Brahmins, who had managed to reserve everything for themselves for quite a few centuries. The revolt against the Brahmins, which goes back many decades, had gone far enough to make the Brahmins in many places the victims of considerable counter-discrimination, forcing many of them to migrate elsewhere or even to change *their* names to something less obviously Brahmin in order to escape some of the exclusions practiced against them. In Mysore, for example, from 1921 to 1959, Brahmins could hold only three out of every ten government jobs. Revised rules issued in 1961 reserved a total of 64 percent of all jobs in the state for the Scheduled Castes, Tribes, and Other Backward Classes. Similar quotas operated against the Brahmins in Andhra, Madras, and Kerala.[23] A government commission in 1955 continued to defend the use of caste as the criterion for backwardness, although at the last moment its chairman changed his mind, denounced the practice, and said some other way had to be found to deal with the problem.

This issue caused a great confusion of political fights and court cases. The Supreme Court, denouncing some of these state arrangements as "a fraud on the Constitution," began pulling in the reins on what threatened to become a runaway absurdity imperiling the entire government program.[24] The

23 Cf. M. N. Srinivas, "Pursuit of Equality," *Times Survey of India*, Jan. 26, 1962; also his "Changing Institutions and Values in Modern India," *Economic Weekly Annual Review*, February, 1962.

24 Cf. Donald E. Smith, *India as a Secular State*, Princeton, 1963, pp. 316ff; *Report of the Backward Classes Commission*, New Delhi, 1956. For an examination of the legal and judicial aspects of this matter, see the studies by Marc Galanter: "Equality and 'Protective Discrimination' in India," *Rutgers Law Review*, XVI:1, Fall, 1961; "The Problem of Group Membership: Some Reflections on the Judicial View of Indian Society," *The Journal of the Indian Law Institute*, IV:3, July-Sept. 1962; "Law and Caste in Modern India," *Asian Survey*, III:11, Nov. 1963.

Central Government and many of the states began to move to-ward imposing economic rather than caste criteria for defining "backwardness." These took effect during 1963, with cutoff points at annual incomes of R1,000 to R1,500 ($210 to $315) coming into more general use to screen out undeserving re-cipients of government help. "Four states in the south still have quotas in government jobs for 'Other Backward Classes,'" a high Home Ministry official in New Delhi told me. He went on:

"Backward" seems to have a special meaning down there. There is a stigma attached to being Scheduled Caste, but it was fine to get the money without the stigma simply by being "OBC." Everybody wanted to be "OBC" including the dominant groups in some states. Mysore has never had a chief minister who was not a Lingayat, a group whose name was removed from the "Backward" list, but they insisted and succeeded in getting it restored. On the other hand, you have the Anglo-Indians, who also got benefits but they protested against being called "backward." They wanted to get rid of this description while, of course, keeping the benefits.

None of this confusion and controversy over who else was "backward" affected the status of the Scheduled Castes and Tribes. No one could challenge *their* backwardness and very few of them in any case had broken through the income floor fixed as the bottom limit. The national and state pro-grams were designed primarily to help them. Listed specif-ically by caste, they remained the prime targets of the special welfare programs and the beneficiaries of the quota system of reserved places in government jobs of all kinds and at all levels.

This Indian system of reverse discrimination, sometimes called "progressive discrimination," is all but unique. The nearest counterpart I know of is operating in Malaya, with some rather important differences. In Malaya the politically dominant Malays are maintaining a quota system for their own people, Malays being favored four to one in certain categories of government appointments and university scholarships. This is intended to correct the imbalance created by Malay backwardness and the much higher levels of education and competence among the politically subordinate Chinese and Indian citizens of the country. In Cyprus, quotas were set to apportion government posts between the mutually hostile majority Greek and minority Turkish Cypriots as part of the abortive effort to see if these two groups could co-exist peacefully on their small island. In the United States there have been quotas favoring war veterans in some kinds of government employment. But India is the only country where government employment quotas and educational benefits have been established right across the board in order to help speed the social and economic elevation of specific groups from the lowest levels of the country's population.

In the central government services in India, the quota for the Scheduled Castes in jobs filled by competitive examination is 12½ percent (5 percent for Scheduled Tribesmen) and 16⅔ percent in all other jobs filled simply by appointment. The states operate on variations of these percentages according to differences in their local population figures. In theory, when jobs are filled from examination lists, the places go to the top competitors on the general list until the 12½ percent level is reached, at which point the remaining places go to the Scheduled Caste competitors with passing scores no matter how much lower these scores might be. In fact, up to now in government white collar jobs the actual percentages of ex-Untouchables employed has fallen far short of the quotas. In 1963 they were only 1 to 7 percent filled. Government spokesmen say they cannot fill the quotas because there are too few qualified applicants. Scheduled Caste

spokesmen complain that the real reason is continuing discrimination, especially in cases where a personal interview
is part of the appointment procedure and caste Hindu inter-
viewers are able to exercise their prejudices. This argument
goes on about jobs in the white collar categories only. At the
lowest levels of manual or menial work, of course, the quotas
are filled without difficulty.

The most recent figures available show the employment
position in the central government services as it was stated
to be on January 1, 1963. As given by the Commissioner
for Scheduled Castes and Tribes,[25] these figures show a total
of 329,046 ex-Untouchables employed in these services out of
a total of over 2,300,000. The report adds that it was impossible to get a comparable total for those employed in the
state services.

The top of the crop in the government are the members
of the "I.A.S." or Indian Administrative Services, heirs to
the highly prestigious "I.C.S." or Indian Civil Service of
the British time. These are the top administrative posts,
occupied at the most senior levels always by Englishmen in
the old days, and since independence, of course, by Indians,
as senior administrators and secretaries in the ministries and
departments of the government. In 1963 there were 18,021
members of the I.A.S. Of these 237, or 1.3 percent, were
ex-Untouchables. In 1962, the quota posts for Scheduled
Caste applicants, 22 positions, were filled for the first time,
and the same thing happened with the 11 positions open by
quota in 1963. This marked a real turning point, my Home
Ministry informant told me, for they showed that enough
educated ex-Untouchables were now beginning to come out
of the universities to produce enough applicants with the

[25] Supplied to the writer in mid-1964 from the figures being prepared for
the Commissioner's report for 1962–63.

necessary qualifications. In 1961–62, 6,000 applicants, including more than 600 with 1st class degrees, took examinations for the 99 posts that were going. The competition was extremely close, with a margin of 200 points or "marks" out of a top possible score of 1,800 separating the lowest man on the general list from the top man on the Scheduled Caste list. At the narrowest point, this difference was a margin of only about 10 percent, he remarked, but as you moved on down the list, the margin widened and the difference between top man and low man became painfully wide. The successful candidates go into the ministries as third secretaries and the best of them will rise in 20 years or so to the top posts. "We are worried about this difference in quality," he said. "The effect on administration won't be visible for some years to come, but it will appear." The government actually goes to some lengths to help ex-Untouchables qualify for this top service, maintaining two coaching centers where candidates work for a fully supported year to prepare themselves for the examination.

The class 2 category of Indian government servants is the grade that leads to positions that have some executive responsibility plus a heavy portion of plain clerical work. As of January 1, 1963, there were 28,968 such officials in the service of the central government and of these 761, or 2.6 percent, were members of the Scheduled Castes. Class 3 is simple clerical work carried on by the lowest grade of white collar civil servants of whom there were 1,131,760 in the service on that date, and of these 79,336, or 7 percent, were ex-Untouchables. Class 4 consists mainly of manual workers and plain laborers in the government's agencies and enterprises, as well as the great masses of messengers, menials, and flunkeys who inhabit the corridors of all Indian government buildings and who are still universally called "peons" as they were in the British time. The total of such workers is

1,061,646, and of these 186,481, or better than 17.5 percent, are ex-Untouchables. It was rather striking to find, going through these figures, that just as there are four great Varna or castes in the caste system, and then the Untouchables as a fifth group of but not in the system, the Indian government's services are similarly organized in these four main classes, plus the sweepers, who are listed quite separately outside the regular classifications, the tables in the record showing a separate group of 68,950 sweepers, of whom 62,231, a whacking non-quota 90 percent, are listed as ex-Untouchables.

Some of the statistics brought together in Indian government reports can be quite obscure. Aside from those I have just quoted, for example, there is quite another set which says there were 356,037 registrations of Scheduled Caste applicants in the Employment Exchanges during 1961, and that of these only 49,976 were actually placed in jobs. The status of those who were not placed is not clear and there would be no way at all of knowing, from these tables, the educational levels involved in these transactions. Another set of figures— these all appear in the Appendices to the report of the Commissioner for Scheduled Castes and Tribes—indicates that in 1961 the Employment Exchanges were "notified" of 445,143 vacancies in central government and state jobs and 344,830 by "other employers"—not otherwise identified—making a grand total of 789,973. Of this great mass of jobs, the table says, only 12,977 were "notified as reserved for the Scheduled Castes" and of these only 5,637 were filled. It would take much more study than I was able to give them to know what these figures mean or how to reconcile one table with another.[26]

Out of all this, however, certain large summary facts do

<hr>

[26] Cf. *Report of Commissioner*, 1961–62, Appendix XXXIV, p. 95.

emerge clearly enough even if they cannot be made precise as to numbers. At the bottom of the widening pyramid of mass education in India, the ex-Untouchables, like Indians in general, are becoming literate at the rate of many millions of people every year, generating new but incalculable pressures for change in the society as a whole. At the top of the pyramid, among the 1,000,000 who are getting higher education, there are 55,000 ex-Untouchables and this number is also rising steeply each year. To the figure of some 330,000 ex-Untouchables who now hold central government jobs at all levels, one has to add unknown totals for teachers and for all who are working for the states, the municipalities, and the districts. Some figure has to be added in here also for the number of ex-Untouchables who have moved from the old sub-menial occupations into more or less semi-skilled industrial jobs in the private and public sectors of the economy. Counting only job-holding adults, all those who fall under these various headings might be guessed to be in the neighborhood of a million people. If we count in the children of these ex-Untouchables who are in school, we arrive at a total of nearly six million human beings who are by these means coming up out of the lowest estate into which any people have ever fallen anywhere at any time in human history, and are now moving into some new condition of life.

The program of special help and job quotas which has been making this possible has been operating now for not quite 15 years. As we have already indicated, it is now legally fixed to last until 1970. Many good people, both ex-Untouchables and caste Hindus, are worried about it. They are afraid the "special" position of the ex-Untouchable will remain and will harden while India's efforts to cope with vast problems continues on into a more and more indefinite future. They see that the great mass of ex-Untouchables is

caught in the same bind as the greater rural mass and will
not be raised out of poverty and backwardness any faster
than the several hundred million other inhabitants of India's
villages. The caste system is, if anything, more powerful in
the new India than it was in the old, having become the core
of the new politics. It remains, as scholar M. N. Srinivas
has said, "an institution of prodigious strength; it will take
a lot of beating before it will die." [27] Even as far as Untouchability itself is concerned, change is so hard to see among the
rural masses that real improvement at the present rate will
take, it seems, forever. But at least two things are working
the other way. The first is the process of urbanization and
industrialization which by its very nature runs against the
writ of caste. Halting as it may be, this process is creating a
growing layer of modernizing people in the top crust of
Indian society and such people cannot and will not be
squeezed indefinitely into molds of the past. The second
is that the program of special benefits and opportunities for
ex-Untouchables has produced a counterpart layer of educated modernizers right off the top of the lowest group of
all in the Indian mass.

These people, one million or six million as you count
them, are coming up out of the old pits and troughs. They
are living in cities, coming into new kinds of employment,
discovering new ways of life, and raising children from new
and much higher thresholds. They are still barely scratching
their way along this rough but rising slope, but they are on
their way up and out of the slime from which they came
and in which most of their kith and kin still live. There is
much to be glimpsed of what is happening to these individuals
and there are obviously many problems and tensions created
by the complicated experience through which they are pass-

[27] *Report of Seminar on Casteism*, etc., p. 133. See also Selig S. Harrison,
India: The Most Dangerous Decades. Princeton. 1960

ing. But one thing at least is certain: they would not be where they are and would not be having these experiences if it were not for the special help and preferences fixed by law in their behalf. Even with all the laws and all the earnest exhortation from well-meaning caste Hindu reformers, the changes in the "hearts and minds of men" among caste Hindus in India have not been exactly spectacular. I do not think anybody can be under any illusion as to what the picture would be now if these ex-Untouchables had to depend not on these legally-enforced advantages but only on the voluntary goodwill of caste Hindus. Hardly a fraction of the present progress would have been made. This fact should never be allowed to slip out of sight as one moves on to consider some of the problems and conflicts created by this unique experiment of discrimination-in-reverse.

8. THE PRICE OF PREFERENCE

The whole of this experience is undercut by at least one painful anomaly. All good Indian liberals have long said they wanted, like Gandhi, to reform the caste system, or like Nehru to abolish it. But almost everything that has happened in the development of the new politics since Indian independence has served not to weaken or eliminate caste but to strengthen it. In the effort to help the ex-Untouchables, this counter-effect has been quite explicit. All the programs and quotas are intended to help the ex-Untouchable shed his identity, but the effect has been to make this identity more visible than ever. The idea is to root out this form of casteism and blot out the ignominy of this past status. But the individual who seeks help in getting rid of his identity must proclaim it. He wants to get away from his past, but he must announce it. He must write it down, he must, indeed, prove it by supplying a properly attested certificate to show that he is what the government is presumably trying to help him escape from being. He has to certify that he is an ex-Untouchable before the government can help him to become something else.

This is a very literal matter, not only bureaucratic but "reasonable." When an ex-Untouchable seeks a scholarship or a quota position in admission or employment, he has to establish his ex-Untouchability. This is done by submitting a certificate on a form supplied by the government. Until a year or so ago, this form required the applicant to indicate his "community." It began to appear, however, that these benefits were good enough to attract some of the officially undeserving as well as the deserving poor. The Commissioner for Scheduled Castes and Tribes in his Report for 1961–62 pointed out the danger of "certain persons belonging to some non-Scheduled Caste 'communities' and having surnames similar to those of some of the Scheduled Castes, trying to avail of benefits provided especially for Scheduled Caste persons." Hence the language of the certificate was ordered changed: "This ambiguity can be avoided if the term 'community' used in the form of certificate prescribed by the Government of India . . . is replaced by the words 'Caste [or] Tribe.' " [28] Nobody can now loosely affirm ex-Untouchable status; he has to pin it down with hard particulars. In this way, the anomalies multiply and even grow absurd. To lose himself in the larger society, the ex-Untouchable has to mark himself out in a way no other kind of person must do. To get rid of his outcaste status, he has to name his caste.

Since these benefits are distributed strictly by the criterion of caste (or to get technical, the criterion of belonging to a casteless caste), obviously all the beneficiaries have to be properly sorted out and identified. As noted earlier, the government has expressed its nominal anti-casteism in a most literally nominal way, by eliminating caste designations from all official records. Because of the formal position of the Congress movement on this point, the last census to list people by caste was the census of 1931. But now, precisely because there are these special programs for the benefit of the Scheduled Castes and Tribes, the government needs to know which ones they are. So they became the exceptions and in the 1961 census they, and they alone, were listed by caste. This was done for the creditable purpose of making sure that the benefits and quotas were distributed to those for whom

28 *Report*, 1961–62, p. 5.

they were intended. The effect, again, was to make every Scheduled Caste person a more clearly marked man than any other kind of man in the whole country.

This built-in contradiction has dogged almost every aspect of these well-meant programs. The modest efforts to provide better housing for some Scheduled Caste villagers or to distribute some land to the landless have had the effect usually of separating them even more than they were separated before. It was some years before someone pointed out that no law had been passed against segregation of the ex-Untouchables, and that much of the welfare effort actually increased and deepened their separateness. Thus in the first years, in the anxiety to help them get the benefits of education, many separate schools were established for the Scheduled Castes, and in many places separate hostels were built for these separate students to live in. The record is full of strictures and misgivings about benefits that served only to "crystallize the feeling of separateness," [29] an outcome not without echoes of similar experiences affecting Negroes in the United States. One result of these criticisms was the fixing of special quotas for admitting Scheduled Caste students at some universities to the "general hostels" intended for all, but then this required additional stipends, for the separate hostels were free and the general hostels were not. As one specialist pointed out some time back, "The policy of giving relief by caste groups has increased their caste immobility." [30]

The need to be identified and labeled in order to be helped relentlessly pursues the individual all the way through school and later out into the world. At the school stage an ex-Untouchable student can and often does make his way, if he is bold about it, into some more casually free associa-

[29] *Report of Seminar on Casteism*, p. 40.
[30] *Ibid.*

tion with fellow students who are caste Hindus, and in this day-to-day association the question of caste might simply never come up. It involves going together to classes, perhaps a sharing of some amusements, or even daily life in the hostel. At this casual level—where no family visiting or other intimacies get involved—no one may raise the question of caste, least of all the ex-Untouchable. But then comes the day when the scholarship list comes out and is posted on the bulletin board. My notes of talks with students are liberally dotted with the moments of painful discovery that took place standing that day in front of that bulletin board scanning that list. A typical experience:

A Brahmin friend of mine did not think I was Scheduled Caste because I never told him. We used to go all about together. At the end of the year came the notice of the scholarships. "Hey," he said to me in surprise, "you belong to the Scheduled Caste?" I said yes. He didn't say anything. So I said: "Do you feel it?" He replied: "Oh, no, that's all changed." We still go together as before, but the feelings are there, at the roots.

This experience strikes doubly at those Mahars in Maharashtra who followed Ambedkar and became Buddhists. As usual, a firm figure is hard to come by but it is said that more than 2,000,000 Mahars became Buddhists in order to free themselves from the stigma of Untouchability they had to bear as Hindus. The government authorities, all Hindus, early ruled—perhaps not without a touch of malice—that "no person who professes a religion different from Hinduism shall be deemed to be a member of the Scheduled Castes." This is a matter, as we shall have occasion to note later, that also involved Christians and Muslims and caused quite some agitation. In Maharashtra, where they had some political weight, the state benefits were restored to the "Neo-Buddhists," as these ex-Untouchables were sometimes called. But to get the more important central government assistance anybody who privately thought of himself as a "Buddhist" still had to declare himself formally and officially to be a member of the Scheduled Castes in order to qualify. Ambedkar may have had this contingency in mind when he suggested at one point that people in this category be called "statutory Hindus" in order to safeguard their privileges, but no one took up his suggestion which, indeed, he may only have made ironically. In any case, this added a certain moral dilemma to all the other dilemmas of the Mahar-Buddhist, or of any ex-Untouchable who had to declare himself formally a member of the group from which he wanted so profoundly to escape. I cannot offer any general remark about their feelings on this score. Answers about it usually came in straightforward rationalizations with little or no indication of pain or conflict. Typically:

My father was converted to Buddhism. But I am not. I don't have to convert until I am older. If I write down Buddhist, I get only a freeship [exemption from fees] but if I write down Hindu and Mahar, I get a scholarship. So I write down Hindu and Mahar.

Occasionally there would be more of a glimpse of ambivalence:

By conviction I'm a Buddhist, but if I became a Buddhist openly, I wouldn't get scholarships. . . . There *are* stauncher ones who stick to principle and say what they are. Each person must settle this for himself. After Dr. Ambedkar died, there has been no one to guide the people and tell them what to do.

In one young man strong feelings flashed when this came up. He was a twenty-year-old undergraduate who in an hour's talk veered—or perhaps zigzagged is the word—through several levels of response to this particular conflict. His father was a man who "passed" successfully by going to a distant city to work for a foreign firm, but the boy was sent all the way back to Bombay for his higher education because there he could safely claim his benefits as a member of a Scheduled Caste.

My father became a Buddhist in honor of Ambedkar but could not ever say so openly. I became a Buddhist too, but only orally, because on the forms you have to write down Scheduled Caste. If you are Buddhist, you can't get the scholarship. But I am proud to follow Ambedkar! Being Scheduled Caste causes inferiority in our minds. To be Buddhist, it makes me feel free!

His words were tumbling out over each other. When he paused I asked how, then, it felt to put "Scheduled Caste" down on the form. He pulled his face into a sudden hard grimace. "It is for this reason I *hate* this government," he said fiercely. "I have hatred for it. It says it makes no difference among any religions, but it supports Hinduism. It *makes* me put down Scheduled Caste on the form! If I am asked what I am, I like to say, 'I'm Buddhist. I have no community at all.' This does happen and I say I am Buddhist, and people then take me as an inferior. 'Oh,' they say, 'you are a Mahar Buddhist,' ridiculing us for this, and I say, 'No! We are not Mahar, we are *Buddhist!*'" A few minutes later, in much more relaxed tones, he was saying:

I want to be an engineer. I finished my examinations today and I did pretty well, I think. I will get scholarships, monetary help. We are not obliged to the government for this. For thousands of years the Hindus kept us downtrodden and now we need this help. They have to compensate us for the damage done to our community. For this you have to put down "Scheduled Caste." This is a technical difficulty. After I finish my education, I will tell them I am a Buddhist and I will be proud to tell it. I won't allow any children of *mine* to take scholarships from the government.

I will pay for it all myself. My father had to provide for all of his family and he did not have enough, but I will have R3,000 or R4,000 [$630 or $840] a month. I will tell my children they are *Buddhist*. I won't tell them about being Mahars. I will make them bold enough to say to the Hindus they are *Buddhists*, to say this to these Hindus who *force* us to say we are Scheduled Caste!

The idea that later on, when one's education was done, one would be free at last of the hated identification was voiced more than once. But this did not take account of some of the further facts of life. In government service the Scheduled Caste label had to be kept in view not only for appointment to a job but also, over time, for promotions up through the grades of service. A man's stake in his ex-Untouchable identity remains high right on into his working years wherever his chances for betterment continue to be based on his "rights" as an ex-Untouchable rather than on any of his individual merits. I found this to be a matter of some feeling among many of the persons I met, but a much more relaxed view of it was put to me by Vimal Chandra, Deputy Commissioner for Scheduled Castes and Tribes, who said:

I think this is disappearing. The safeguards have brought out self-respect and the fear of being ashamed is disappearing. The Scheduled Caste man now has things he is entitled to as a "right" and I don't think the average Scheduled Caste man gives two thoughts to the problems in this. He doesn't even think about them. He was a man in a big pit and now he's been helped out of it. That's all that counts. A Scheduled Caste man had no self-respect at all 25 years ago. He was a complete nobody. But now he's something. He is not concerned with whether he came up by merit. It is simply that he's now better off than his father was. So he demands a place. He is a more self-respecting man than he ever could be before. There is some resentment of this from caste Hindu competitors, but this cannot be helped. . . . You've got to realize that most of these people would not have come up otherwise at all. The community as a whole I think has rationalized this as a "right" and repressed this feeling of inner loss through its special status. People like to get benefits now. Before there was a tendency to conceal in order to avoid difficulties, but the benefits are an attraction.... So all who are concerned have to identify themselves. This is, after all, even a way of getting into Parliament! Why, a caste Hindu fellow said to me the other day: "Tell me, how can I get into the Scheduled Castes?" I said laughing: "You'll have to die to do it!" We are going to begin to have problems now because we are producing more educated people than jobs. This is true for people in general and it is beginning to apply to the Scheduled Castes too.

Caste Hindu responses to these improvements in the status of ex-Untouchables have been mixed and unsurprisingly seem to depend on just how close to the whole thing a caste Hindu gets. Up in the busy cosmopolitan world of leaders and pundits, it is dealt with in more or less airy generalizations. If my own friends and acquaintances are any fair indication—and I think they are—they never see an ex-Untouchable, as far as they know, unless they glimpse a scavenger or sweeper at work and the question of his identity and his place in the scheme of things catches for an instant at some edge of their minds. They say all the right things about it, but they are busy with other great affairs. Academics who possibly come into contact with Scheduled Caste students might remark on how "aggressive" they are, and what poor students. Their contact is minimal and, among those I met, their interest not great.

Out in the villages, there have been some rather violent reactions by caste Hindus when members of the Scheduled Castes have tried to assert their new rights or to act in some intolerably independent way, such as trying to enter the temples, use the wells, or begin to participate in local bodies, as they have, in every case, the full right to do. There have been riots and shootings over episodes like this and a number of ex-Untouchables have been killed in these affairs.[31] Many more, as the record of offenses and complaints shows, have been beaten by caste Hindu village goons even for such trespasses as having musicians at a wedding. At the faster-moving outer edge of advancement, however, there has apparently been an impressive degree of acceptance by caste Hindus of the special preferences given to the Scheduled Castes. This is partly because Indians do commonly accept what they are ordered by higher authority to accept and partly because, as some caste Hindus said, there is a tacit acknowledgment of past injustices that do have to be righted somehow. But here again, these lofty feelings are much more likely to be expressed by a caste Hindu who is good and far from the problem himself. One does not imagine great surges of benevolent goodwill rising in the breast of a person crowded out of a desirable government job by competitors scoring as much as 10 percent or more lower on the examination than he did. Heavy strains appeared quite early in the fabric of this acceptance. This grew even more visible when the Supreme Court in 1961 affirmed a ruling that the quota system could be applied not merely to appointments but also to promotions. This ruling came out of a case brought by a railway employee in Madras and although the court said the percentages could be applied to promotions as a matter of policy and not of law, ex-Untouchables throughout government service took it as a mandate and the issue caused much friction between them and their caste Hindu fellow employees and much difficulty for the administration, where there are some responsible officials who do worry over the problems of establishing and maintaining some appropriate level of efficiency. The present practice, I was told at the Home Ministry, is to promote automatically by the percentages in

---

[31] See Report of Seminar on Casteism, etc., p. 194.

Class 3 (clerical) and Class 4 (manual and menial) services, but not in Classes 1 or 2 where rising executive responsibilities go with advancement.

The sheer matter of numbers, as Vimal Chandra and others pointed out, is beginning to impose itself on the whole situation. In recent years the government expanded at a rapid rate but it obviously cannot go on expanding indefinitely. At the same time, the number of Scheduled Caste applicants above the manual and menial levels was never pressingly high and those who qualified could be absorbed at relatively low cost to caste Hindu competitors; as we have seen, through 1963, the quota that allowed up to 12½ percent was only 1 to 7 percent filled. But the ex-Untouchables are beginning to come up now in much greater numbers. More and more quota jobs at the top level are being filled for the first time, and the competition is getting sharper, not only among all applicants, but among Scheduled Caste applicants themselves. One hears commonly of ex-Untouchables taking examination after examination in various government services year after year until they finally reach a place where they can squeak through to a job. Everyone predicts that the going will get tougher, the competition harsher, the frictions greater. It would be a bit premature, however, to begin feeling sorry for the caste Hindu who loses by discrimination that favors the ex-Untouchable. In this relationship, the danger of the caste Hindu losing his top-dog status is nil and the ex-Untouchable remains a man who still has the burdens of all the centuries to shed. The question is not the cost of this reform to the caste Hindus, but the price the ex-Untouchables have to pay for what they gain.

Much of what appears in this experience blends readily into the pattern of dependency that is such a large part of the whole design of Indian life. Addressing an audience of ear-

nestly interested caste Hindus nearly ten years ago, Jagjivan
Ram, for many years the only Scheduled Caste minister in the
cabinet, said that the former Untouchables needed these special rights because without them discrimination and disability
would persist, and that without them it would simply be left
to caste Hindus "to assume the role of benevolent guardians
who must determine how their wards must grow and de-
velop." [32] As things have worked out, this is actually the role
that caste Hindus have played anyway. Benevolence and dependency is the essential quality of the whole program, laws
and all, with the ex-Untouchables becoming more or less
docile wards who aggravate their caste Hindu benefactors and
mentors by not doing enough to reform themselves and who
are seen as "overaggressive" if they insist too strongly on their
"rights" and are insufficiently grateful for the state's largesse.

These relationships are particularly visible in the sphere
of politics. Ever since Gandhi fasted Ambedkar out of an
independent political identity for the Untouchables in 1932
and then launched his program of reform by exhortation,
welfare, and uplift, the Congress Party has kept the Scheduled
Castes quite largely under its influence and control. In the
various states Congress politics has become mainly a matter
of caste combinations. As the party in power, Congress leadership groups sit astride all roads leading to office, job, preferred
position. The men to occupy the reserved seats in the legislature are hand picked for the job, a fat plum for whoever gets
it and a lot to jeopardize by being a troublemaker. Any ex-
Untouchable can stand, of course, for one of the general seats,
but this is not easy to do, requiring both a strongly independent spirit and an independent source of political strength,
neither being easy for an ex-Untouchable to find. As the
source of all benefits, the Congress Party has largely kept the
allegiance of the ex-Untouchables. There is no strong in-

[32] *Report of Seminar*, p. 37.

dependent political current among them and it is striking to see how little headway has been made among them by either the Socialists or Communists, the self-nominated natural leaders of all underdogs. The Socialists, perennially split among themselves, have been no more successful in winning the support of the ex-Untouchable poor than of the Indian poor in general. The Communists, stronger but also usually split into factions, have won some Scheduled Caste support, as in Andhra and Kerala, but more as part of a rather complicated game of local caste politics than as a serious political mobilization of any durability.[33] The Congress politicians of the Scheduled Castes whom I met tended to be rather carefully defensive when they talked of these things, never professing to be "satisfied," but never being too critical either. A blunter oppositionist view was put to me by young Maurya, the Ambedkarite fromUttar Pradesh who holds not a reserved but a general seat, incidentally, thanks to a fortuitous anti-Congress alliance in his district. Maurya was the only ex-Untouchable I encountered who flatly and explicitly opposed the whole program of special reservations and benefits for the Scheduled Castes. He said:

This system does the Scheduled Castes no good because the people in the reserved seats belong to the party in power and are often incapable persons. Although they are educated, they dare not speak out against the party in power. They do not represent their people to the party and government, but represent the party in power to their people. They do not fight their people's cause. As for the school benefits, we do not need them in this form either. If there is free compulsory education for all, then every person will have access to it anyway. In higher education let scholarships be given where there is economic need. All our people are poor and the party in power is not solving the problems of poverty. As for the quotas in government service, these are only

[33] See Harrison, *India: The Most Dangerous Decades*, Chap. VI.

one to three percent filled and they take our best people. In government service, the educated people are kept out of politics and we are left with illiterate workers. We say end these reservations. They are just a way of keeping the weaker section weak, to keep them subject to the party in power.

It was often said both by caste Hindus and ex-Untouchables that the new generation of young people moving up along this path of preferment to improved positions are intent only on their own self-improvement and do not care about "social work" (which in India means work for the community as distinct from work for oneself) or politics. A senior Scheduled Caste Congress politician had some unhappy things to say about the younger generation:

Unfortunately the passion for education is lacking. We have so many failures. The students are not as keen as the older ones because they haven't really felt Untouchability. In politics, it is their lot that there is nothing exact to be done while we had so much to do. Politics has become a game of clever manipulation, not the work of really deserving or dedicated men. Motivation is more or less absent. You rarely come across men keen to *do* something. They are mostly drawn in just to stand for the election. They don't really care. They are set up for it by the party. Once they come in, of course, they don't want to go out.

No new Ambedkars are appearing among the young, but a mass of self-engrossed people who are quickly and easily satisfied with the small gains they can win for themselves. This may be natural enough in the circumstances, but there are many who look forward with foreboding to the next stage of things. A prominent caste Hindu leader, a weary veteran of Indian politics, told me:

Now we have the large influx of Scheduled Castes in the universities. To what extent they will throw up new people we won't know for a time. It is simply not visible now. I think it unlikely for them to move into politics. They are interested in jobs, getting fed, a better living. On the whole, so far, they have followed Congress, but when things get difficult, this will change. They will join the floating mass of unemployed, some of whom are already supporting regional and linguistic extremism, as in the Dravidian movement in Madras. In Kerala they have gone with the Communists. In Bengal they are simply floating disoriented people. The young people getting educated are being separated from the rest of their people. The mass consists of the less enterprising who are stuck in the mud, and where the educated ones will go, no one knows.

Another discouraged caste Hindu politician said:

Today they are quite easily won over, a little money, a little position. This is what happens to most of them. They end up in minor jobs, not trying to fight the caste system, but trying to get individual status, trying to get accepted in the higher castes. Maybe after they have had education in larger numbers and find they cannot get absorbed into the higher castes and also find themselves unemployed, they will become more revolutionary.

Maurya, the plain-speaking oppositionist, said:

When a man is taken into government service, he becomes a member of another class. He stops mingling with Scheduled Caste people. He becomes a victim of the caste system in a new way. In the new circle he is looked down on. So he ends up nowhere.

9. THE SEMI-LIMBO

As the educated ex-Untouchables pull up and away from the sodden bleakness of their past estate, they do not quite get *nowhere,* but neither do they reach *somewhere.* They are people who want above all to become different from what they were and what their fathers were. They want to leave all that behind, to forget it, to blot it out, but they come into a situation where too little is changing too slowly; a society still governed by caste does not allow them to abandon their past, to forget it, to blot it all out. What they move into becomes a kind of semi-limbo.

Behind them a widening distance opens between them and the rest of their community, even their closest kin. This happens to those raised in the city and even more to those who come up in the village. One of the I.A.S. aspirants at the coaching school in Bangalore, a stocky, nearly jet-black young man, an Ada-Andhra from a village called Laddigan, described what it was like when he went home:

When I go back, they feel different toward me, even though I treat them all as equal to me. But I find I can only stay there two or three days. I need paper and books. I can't get anything there. Our house is a dilapidated house. Here I live in a room with friends and I eat in restaurants and I have friends to talk to. In the village I have no friends to talk to, no books to read, no papers to see. In our district very few children go to school. The parents are ignorant, there is no encouragement, no one insists. I talk about welfare. I tell things about myself to my mother.

There is some reserve between father and son. Normally sons won't move freely with their fathers, only rarely do they talk freely. I talk to my father and brother only about family affairs. They are proud of me when I come, they celebrate and get me things, prepare special food, and insist on my staying longer.

In Bombay our airline pilot friend, Khadtale, took us one evening to have tea at the home of a friend of his, a senior government official, an ex-Untouchable who had been able to move his family of four daughters and two sons to a middle-class apartment block where they lived in plain but comfortable style. The people this man had left behind him as he moved up were very much on his mind because, it appeared, they were very much on his back. "We educated people form a separate group," he said. "We are seen as too high above the others." His voice began to take on a sharper edge. "We can't really bring *all* of them up!" He sighed and went on: "We cannot really get ahead. If we do not stay with them, then we are treated as outcasts by them, we become people who go on and get ahead, and leave them behind, when we should be *with* them. But if we try to do this and satisfy them, then we can't bring our own families out ahead." He looked around the modest room in which we were sitting. "We wouldn't even be able to change our place of living," he said. "Our poorer relatives say these things. We cannot satisfy *all* of them!" These feelings, apparently common in families from which some members have risen, are being exploited, he said, by some politicians within the group. "They side with the families against the educated ones," he said. "They criticize the educated for remaining away from their society. This is partly true, but partly it is jealousy, envy, and partly propaganda. There is very little opportunity to mix with our society. I have a brother who is farming and another brother who works in a machine shop and my sister's husband works for the railway. When would I mix with them?"

He felt generally unhappy about all the people below, feeling that the drive for advancement was disappearing and that people were descending into a new kind of morass of their own making:

The majority of people are now not as eager to learn as we were when we were young. They give up after the 4th standard. Education is free up to the 7th standard and yet we find working people with children not going to school, even in the cities. When I came to Bombay in 1940, every parent wanted his children to have education. But now parents send their children out on dirty business, begging, crime, illicit liquor—this happens among working people at the lowest levels who are making maybe R100 or R150 a month. Those who are educated feel frustrated about getting ahead, and the poorer people feel they can't afford education. The trend is against more education, I think. The mass has no power of thinking, no firm opinion about things. We are trying to do something for the masses but we get no cooperation. Faith in each other is lacking. Whom to follow? Nobody knows. Everybody followed Ambedkar, but now nobody knows whom to follow.

During our conversation we were joined by a neighbor who, it quickly appeared, was also an ex-Untouchable. He had evidently been invited in to have a look at our host's rather unusual visitors. He left after a short while and before long another guest appeared, this one accompanied by his wife. He was a fast-talking man who soon identified himself as a caste Hindu. I assumed that he too had been invited to meet the visiting foreigners and was quite aware of all the elements involved in the situation. There was no sign of awkwardness and the talk went on with hardly a break, continuing about the problems of the Scheduled Castes and coming up in the world. The visitor told us a long story about Untouchability in his village when he was a boy and how his father had told him that these caste distinctions were diminishing. He said: "Caste now counts in the middle class and in the lower classes. In the upper groups it does not matter anymore." I remarked that I had only heard caste Hindus say this sort of thing. Across the table Khadtale nodded with an appreciative smile. Our caste Hindu visitor went on: "In the place of work, caste doesn't come up, but in the place of living it does. Here in India, you know, we go into people's private lives, we ask ever more than we should, all sorts of things. If a man is Scheduled Caste, it will make a difference. People won't show it, but they won't mix as freely, they will keep aloof. To me, to a man like me, it makes no difference, but there are very few like me." We talked about the position in their own apartment block where, our host said, there were 336 tenants and possibly six Scheduled Caste families. Nobody seemed sure how the caste Hindus felt about the Scheduled Caste families because it did not seem to have become very explicit. "It is difficult to get into private apartments," our host said; "if you tell your community, you are refused, or they ask more money." The talk went on for another while and it came time to leave. Our host and Khadtale walked us out to the taxi one of his children had called for us. They were smiling at each other, as though at a private joke. "Mr. So-and-so," our host said, referring to the caste Hindu visitor, "did not know until just now that *we* are Scheduled Caste. It will be interesting to see whether it makes a difference."

In the crowded world where they work at their white collar jobs, the educated ex-Untouchables move daily among masses of caste Hindus, and since these are the people they would rather be *like* than anybody else, they do their best simply to lose themselves in that white-shirted mass. In the great blur of people out on the city streets and in the public places, they can and do appear to be just about like everyone else of their class, and one would think it would be equally easy in the great mazelike offices where the Indian bureaucracy works, and indeed, up to a point, it is. In the busy-busy preoccupation of each one with his own concerns, and the trivialities that pass for talk between desks or over tea or soft drinks in the canteen, the prickly question of one's caste identity might just never arise, especially if one is careful to steer the talk away if it ever threatens to wander in that direction. Friendly associations can be maintained especially if they stay casual, if they are not allowed to carry over too far into the non-working hours, or to get too personal. In this way for a considerable time of every day and in a considerable area of life, one's identity as an ex-Untouchable can be quite largely effaced, or at least kept out of sight. It is not so much a matter of hiding one's caste but more a matter, as one person said, of not announcing it.

But from some accounts I heard, this insulation is fairly thin. In jobs where the competition for appointment or promotion has been sharp, identities are unavoidably known and caste Hindu rivals are often resentful, and show their feelings in all the nasty little ways that the situation readily provides. It is not unknown in some government offices for caste Hindus to insist that ex-Untouchables keep cups or glasses in a separate place away from the common supply. Wherever conflicts arise, mistakes are made, or competence brought into question, the appropriate jibes are ready on the lips of the resentful and the malicious, probably spoken out of one's hearing, or the thought conveyed by a taunting or superior look—and all of this, moreover, might really be there or just be imagined. Or, again, out in the public places, the anonymous surface can be suddenly lacerated and a man can be painfully unsure of what to say, how to react. One story:

Just yesterday I went to Victoria Terminus to book a first-class ticket for my superior. At one window the clerk made his entry on the wrong kind of slip. With that slip I went to purchase the ticket at the booking window and passed it in. The man there said with irritation: "This is the wrong slip." I said I didn't know, that the clerk back there had given it to me. And he said: "These Scheduled Caste people! The government is recruiting people who are not fit for their jobs!" I don't think the first clerk was Scheduled Caste at all, but this one just assumed he was, and he showed his contempt. Somebody had made a mistake and he attributed it to the Scheduled Caste. I felt it. But I didn't say anything.

Another person told me of making a complaint about his telephone service and being shrugged off by a clerk with: "What can we do? We have to hold all these places for the Scheduled Castes!"

By way of response to these slights, an ex-Untouchable can become what is called "aggressive"—which usually means insisting on one's rights, big and small, at every point, or even just being openly resentful of contempt or insult. This is the kind of person that a caste Hindu will sometimes describe as being "proud of being Scheduled Caste." Alternatively, he can choose to draw back into himself, back into the safety of his own group, or his own self, keeping away from all the others as much as he can. But it is best, it seems, to have his identity tacitly known without anybody openly taking note of it. A civil servant of high rank said: "I think the others in my office know that I am Scheduled Caste, but they don't express anything about it. My superior told some of them ... but I have not taken the initiative to explain myself in any way, and I don't want to, because I think it is absolutely unnecessary." Another quite senior official said: "In government I never hid myself. Everyone knew I belonged to the Scheduled Caste but no one showed anything openly about it. . . .

I have high caste friends and they have never shown contempt for me to my face."

At the higher levels of individual achievement it is harder, if not impossible, for an ex-Untouchable not to be well known in the local situation. All the big and little tensions of the new relationships are close to or even at the surface, and constant aggravation keeps the nerve ends sore. You would never have thought this, however, on first encountering Dr. Parvathamma, a poised woman of thirty-five, cool and precise in manner and speech, who occupies the high post of Reader in Sociology at Maharajah College in the University of Mysore. Miss Parvathamma is obviously not a person meant to fit into a blank space in her society. She had three distinctions, each one a problem in India and quite a collection when held all at once by one person. She is in the first place an ex-Untouchable, born a member of the Chalavadi caste in a village of northern Mysore. Secondly, she is a woman. Thirdly, she is a bright woman, bright enough to have risen from grade to grade, scholarship to scholarship, until she took a "double-first" B.A. (meaning first-class degree and first in her class), an M.A. with distinction in Philosophy. Then, with a state award to pursue her studies abroad, she went to Manchester in England, where she earned a doctorate. Back in Mysore she was appointed Reader, a high rank for which many aspirants wait many, many years while serving in the humbler rank of Lecturer. From what I had seen of Indian university life, it seemed clear that Indian academics are even more status-conscious, if that is possible, than American academics, and that friendly camaraderie is not exactly the usual style of life and manners among fellow faculty members. It was not difficult to imagine what it was like for Dr. Parvathamma, an ex-Untouchable in a world of caste, a woman in a world of men, and a woman, moreover, who won double-firsts, distinctions, and a British Ph.D.—qualifications not excessively common among the men who seek places in the Indian academic world. I was able to gather that Dr. Parvathamma does not have a particularly clubby time in her department and that apart from attending official university functions, does not lead a lively social life of any kind. She is still unmarried. She told us that she had come up in a family in which she was left fatherless at quite an early age. She said she had nothing in principle against marriage but that the prospects were not encouraging. "I don't think I can find anyone in my caste," she said. "My educational qualifications stand in the way. As for marrying out of my caste, I don't know. Marriage is still endogamous, and this caste endogamy is the stronghold of the caste system. Among teachers it is possible to inter-dine, even to eat meat together, but to marry out of caste, no! One *has* to be of the right caste." Her most vexing practical problem, it appeared, was getting a place to live.

When I came back here I found it difficult to rent a house. For the first few months I stayed in a hostel while looking for a home for myself. Everywhere they would ask my caste when I was renting. I wouldn't be able to get a place. Then I learned that a doctor in Bangalore had a house here. I went to see him and offered 60 rupees [$12.60] rent for a house that normally gets only 45 rupees [$9.45]. He wrote out a letter of agreement, it was all ready, and then he asked me if I was a Lingayat [the local dominant caste]. I said, true to my conscience, no, I was Scheduled Caste. Then he said he would not rent to me, that he could not overlook the wishes of his friends and family. And this was a doctor, educated in England!

Miss Parvathamma had witnesses with her when this occurred and she promptly brought suit against the man and the case was still pending when we met. She was able thereafter to rent a pleasant bungalow, part of the university's own faculty housing, where she was making her home with her grandmother, an old village lady who hovered in the background during our visit, and a young relative. "I don't see any end to all of this in the next two hundred years," Dr. Parvathamma said, "unless there is some kind of violent revolution, and I have no idea such a thing is possible. The government provides benefits and this is an encouraging thing, but there is cutthroat competition among the Scheduled Castes for these things and the caste Hindus are jealous and resentful. The Scheduled Castes are 99.9 percent ignorant. Only a handful are affected. How are we to benefit from this? I think we will separate ourselves from those who do not benefit and I wouldn't be surprised if this is all that happens."

A Member of Parliament is a man of not inconsiderable status and privilege in New Delhi. A modestly pleasant home in the Parliament block goes with the job and his daily contacts are in the busy world of politics. There are 86 ex-Untouchables in the legislature's two houses. One of them I met is a quiet-spoken, calm man with an unusual touch of humor in him (he is the same one who told me of his pleasure on being received as guest at a meal by caste Hindus in his home district only to find a fellow Chamar waiting outside to get the bowl and glass he had brought for the honored guest to use). He first said that "here in New Delhi no one observes Untouchability," but as we talked on it began to appear that out of his fears for his own pride and his uncertainty about the behavior of others, he still acts as though it were still very much in force. Here is how he spoke of his life in the capital:

Sometimes we get invited out, but most often I avoid it, because I know *they* feel it very much and just invite me as a formality. Suppose there is a marriage of a daughter of an upper caste friend. He will invite me, and I have to send a gift, but I avoid going. It *could* happen that they would give me some kind of a separate meal, and I would resent it and be angry, and would make a scandal there. So I don't go. Sometimes I do go, but only to the houses of very trusted people. And I do go, of course, to official functions, like tea parties or "at homes" of other officials. There are friends I know won't practice untouchability in their homes here in New Delhi, but it is in my mind that at their homes back in the villages, they could not treat me like this. This troubles me because of all the experiences of my life. And I know their wives feel this more than the men do. They have inherited all these things from their parents, all of them, and they are not easy to overcome.

There are not many places where we all meet. Invitations do not come that often. We go to festivals, or to eat a meal, or to take tea, perhaps three or four times a year. I have been here two months now and have not invited anybody here myself yet this year. I was invited by a caste Hindu during the Holi festival, but I didn't go. I have a Brahmin friend and an Ahir friend. It is getting easier now to invite or to go to others when you are invited, but a few years ago this was still very strange and unusual.

I used to think this was all due to illiteracy, that as soon as people became literate, it would all be automatically removed. But now experience has shown us that it is going to take a long, long time. Even literate people observe caste, so it is going to take a long time. Ideas are moving, but only very slowly.

In all parties, even in the Communist Party, there is a caste system and a basic caste organization. I remember in the first Parliament a man named Anandas, a Madras member of the Communist Party, made a speech in which he criticized caste Hindus for observing Untouchability. His own party took disciplinary action against him because his speech interfered with some of their own other arrangements. He refused to obey the party's orders not to discuss this subject. He was a Scheduled Caste man himself, and he was expelled by the party. No matter whether a man is Congress or Communist, if he's a Brahmin, he will marry his daughter to a Brahmin. It will take a long time for it to be any different.

He too felt much discouraged about the masses of people behind and below him. He did not think there was enough urge among them to change.

We are trying to teach them, we go to them, we tell them all this is man-made and that it's changing, that it's up to them. But we are the educated ones and only five percent of the Scheduled Caste people are literate. The mass of Scheduled Caste people prefer to hear the word from the upper classes, the caste Hindus, instead of taking advice from us, from their own members of the Parliament. If I give them some advice, they'll go to the upper caste people in the community and ask them if what I said was correct. This makes our progress very slow.

Khadtale, the airlines pilot, was too visible and too self-confident a young man to stand very far back in the semi-limbo of this kind of ex-Untouchable life. When he was taken on by Indian Airlines there were congratulatory receptions and publicity and he became something of a public figure, a role he did not mind at all. "Being Scheduled Caste never gets in my way," he said.

It's no problem. The general impression is that the Scheduled Caste person is backward, inefficient, incapable, and gets a job only because he *is* Scheduled Caste. I have heard that some people have said this of me. But I was in fact the best-qualified pilot in the batch taken at that time, two years ago; I had a navigator's license and the best qualifications of any of them, and I know I am still the best-qualified pilot in that group. There is a policy of preference for Scheduled Caste, but this did not apply in my case.

The issue does not come up, even when there is conflict or friction with others.

There are no personal attacks. It has never been thrown up to me by anyone. But then I am particular to see that such occasions do not arise. I don't enter into arguments about caste or religion or politics. I keep out of arguments like that. I think Brahmins do feel a certain prejudice and there are some among my fellow pilots. But we do mix, and face to face, there are no problems. People's attitudes change with financial change. I guess I am now the highest earner in my age group among Scheduled Caste people. I have a government colony home and I am cosmopolitan in every respect.

Khadtale started up pretty much on his own and he traces his feelings of confidence in himself to the shape of some of his early experiences:

Possibly this does not seem such a great change to me because I got into all this so slowly, almost accidentally. In my school days I was a paying student at an orphanage and then I was a teacher there. At that orphange the boys made paper bags and I worked at that too. I was there for three years, up to my matric. I was the only Scheduled Caste boy there. I think I got a certain grooming from that experience. I learned to mix with other communities without differentiating myself from them. It helped me aim for something higher. I'm not boasting, but if a person has a chance to meet with others of a more educated background, it is easier for him to face the difficulties of life. The orphanage people were not well off, but they were all in higher communities. I think I lost my sense of isolation there. From birth we are isolated. We live in our own separate locality and we never get out of it. You get into its routine. I experienced this in my childhood in my home village. I was not allowed to enter temples or use public wells or the public bath. We were completely cut off from the main part of the village.

Khadtale said he started to break out when he was a small boy in primary school and there one day he heard about Ambedkar.

I think I heard the name Ambedkar before I heard of God. After that at school when they said we couldn't take water from the common pot, we just went up and took it. Most of the Scheduled Caste boys got good marks. I myself was always first in primary school. Later my brother who became a government servant in a small town was refused entry into teashops there or to use the public water tap. We brought suit, and now anybody can do those things there.

Even Khadtale, on his way up, went through periods of living in the semi-limbo of the ex-Untouchable, the condition in which one benefits from having one's identity not quite clearly seen.

When I went to school at Kolhapur I was taken to be some kind of Maratha because my name is not clearly a Mahar name. I never said I was Maratha, but I came with a note from a Maratha man, so I was assumed to be Maratha too and I never said differently. This school was 400 miles from my home. A local Scheduled Caste boy was refused admission to the hostel. This was when I was taking the science course after my matric. I took him in with me and he stayed there illegally. At the pilot training school later on, only the principal knew I was Scheduled Caste. The boys with whom I was taking the training had no idea of it. There was no one asking about anybody's community. They all came from higher castes and rich families. I did not really hide that that I was Scheduled Caste, nor did I broadcast it, because if you do, the outlook of people changes and they look down on you as inferior. You know, I think there was one other Scheduled Caste boy in that training group. I think he was a Chamar, but he never let us know, and I am only guessing. He was killed later in an accident.

Khadtale became a Buddhist in 1956, when he had just finished engineering school and was working at the Bombay airport.

That was before I became a pilot, but for the purposes of the record I still maintained that I belonged to the Scheduled Caste. But very shortly now I will change all my records to Buddhist. I was married by Buddhist rites. My wife is Mahar, a matric. We have one son, and *he* will be a Buddhist entirely. He will have *no* caste, *no* community. Now it automatically follows that a Buddhist is a Mahar. But my son will be *just* a Buddhist.

With his pretty young wife and young son, Khadtale lives in a three-room apartment. He tries to manage all his obligations, with the result that his brother and his wife and their children and two other relatives—ten in all—also live in that one apartment. He cheerfully told me he thought this would be only a temporary problem. He is also trying to keep contact with his community because he knows, he said, that he is still bound to the others from among whom he came. He and some of his friends have started a small private effort among themselves to collect money to buy books and to help students in various ways. He thinks more and more education will prepare ex-Untouchables to compete more successfully, and for this he thinks the reservations and other benefits will have to be maintained for some time to come.

I know it goes against the conscience to say you are Scheduled Caste if you are Buddhist, but if you have to do it to get material benefits and to get ahead, what are you going to do—stay in the same old state? The change is for the better. We were rebels without power, like somebody in a jail cell shaking the bars. Now we have got some education and some better means of livelihood, and we mix with other people. We understand that other people are not so bad at heart, they just act out of tradition. At the same time they see us competing, and the idea of our being something inferior is slowly changing. We were in watertight compartments. Suspicious of each other. We have to change this outlook and learn to compete with each other on the same level. Unless we have the power to compete, we will slide back to the same state we were in.

That is why the special facilities must continue. The political reservations haven't helped us much, but the jobs and training have, even though they have not spread among us to the full extent. They will have to continue for some years, and from time to time we'll have to judge what's to be done. But it does become a sort of halfhearted effort. We lack leaders and guidance and I don't know what to put our hope in. Those who get something will try to better themselves. The rest will remain in great difficulty. Even educated people still live in the slums. There are so many things against them. The lower strata people have no future, even in the city, and in the villages, it is still more hopeless. The society is organized on the basis of caste. It has been so for thousands of years. It will be difficult to destroy it unless there is a great intermingling of races and castes.

As for Khadtale himself, he was looking forward to those 4-engined aircraft. "I have just got my foot on the ladder," he said. He was looking up, but not forgetting also to look down.

10. PASSING

Some kind of *passing* has been part of every ex-Untouchable's experience, as so many of our glimpses of these lives have shown. At almost any point of contact with the caste Hindu world, the satisfaction of a man's simplest needs often depended on his readiness to conceal his caste identity and, if need be, to falsify it. We have seen young people concealing their caste to get food and lodging, to win acceptance or at least to avoid rejection. Anyone who moved out of the fixed patterns of the old Untouchable existence soon had to learn how and when to engage in hiding his identity. A man who has managed to rise fairly high recalled that his own first such experience occurred at the initial crucial turning point of his life. A caste Hindu teacher had grown interested in him and took him to a district town 20 miles from their village to take an examination that was going to determine the shape of the rest of his life.

He told me not to say I was of my caste. He was traveling with me and did not want to have any problem at the hostel. He asked me not to tell and instructed me to say I belonged to another caste. So when I was asked, I said I belonged to the Ahir caste, an agricultural caste, very low but not Untouchable. There were three boys who took that examination that day. The other two failed.

Another person well on his way to high professional status recalled:

When I was eight or nine, my father told me: "If anybody inquires about your caste, tell him you belong to the Baria [a higher caste] so that you may not be hindered or insulted." When we went to visit the village, my father used to wear a Parsi gentleman's hat on the train. My brother and I put on khaki uniforms, something like a Boy Scout uniform, and we also wore Parsi caps, so that others would not know we were of the Scheduled Caste. I felt bad and awkward. I couldn't mix freely with other people. It was a hide-and-seek game. My father used to tell us we had to avoid all these things. He was not angry about it; in fact, he used to take pride that nobody questioned his identity or objected to his presence.

Many of those who have moved up in life have naturally continued to find it easier to "pass" in many situations than not to, and, as we have seen, this often meant not falsifying your identity but not proclaiming it either. If in some instances this was pushed to the point where you actually had to give the name of another caste as your own, well, it did not prove so hard to do. There were so many advantages in doing so, and it corresponded to one's deepest desires—"What we want, what we always wanted," said one person, "was to become something else, to be something higher." So wherever it was needful or possible, you would pass, whether while traveling or even, in a more consistent way, at your place of work where what other people did not know could never hurt you. The need to "pass" on a more consistent basis seemed to come most often out of the effort to get better housing. At the lower levels in the big cities, as we have indicated, caste groups tend to live quite separately in sandwiched layers through the great slum tenement blocks. As the economic level rises, some locations still remain caste-bound but more generally nowadays Hindus of various castes will be found living side by side. The higher the scale, the fewer the separations, even for Brahmins. Anybody can get in who has the price—anybody, that is, except an ex-Untouchable. Here the line remains quite rigidly drawn. Better housing will be open where it is public, in government colonies or government-supported apartment block locations. But in most privately owned housing, the ex-Untouchable is likely to be turned away if his identity is known. "That is why many hide their caste," a prominent Bombay ex-Untouchable told me. "They say they are some other caste, even Brahmin, or some say they are Christians or Muslims. 'Why live like a dog in some other place?' they ask."

But there are serious limits to how far and for how long an educated ex-Untouchable can continue to pass successfully in India today. Some have tried to disappear from view entirely, only to be overtaken eventually by the demands of life in a society still dominated by caste. One man who is partially passing himself told me:

You may be able to go up yourself, but you can't take the whole family with you. I know of some people who go away from here and hide their identity entirely and try to solve their problems by themselves. I know one man who worked for a steamship company who hid his identity and called himself by another name. He refused all help to Scheduled Caste people. He would say he just didn't belong to the Scheduled Castes. But then his family grew up and the time came to marry his daughters and he could not find anybody. He had to come back to the community after all to find husbands for them. You can't disappear entirely. There are always relatives and parents, always ceremonies, marriage, and death.

It was death that brought an end to another story of passing told to me:

If a man conceals his caste, sooner or later it is discovered, and then he suffers a lot. There was a Mahar, a contractor who got rich. He told everybody he was a Maratha. He lived in a caste Hindu community and never disclosed his caste. But then his daughter died. The custom is that your relatives must come to prepare the body, not yourself or a stranger. But nobody came. No Marathas came of course. He had cut himself off from his relatives, so they didn't come. Some of his friends and neighbors came and said to him: "How is it nobody is here? Call your nearest relative now, right away!" In desperation he finally called on some of his old people to come to lift the body. When they came, the neighbors recognized them from their clothes, their language, the way they talked, and his caste was disclosed. He suffered. We say to such a man, "You see, you wanted to be a Brahmin or a Maratha, why should we feel sympathy for you?"

Marriage remains the most formidable barrier in the path of anyone who wishes to escape his caste. Intercaste marriage among caste Hindus is less infrequent in India now than it was a generation ago,[34] but such marriages involving Scheduled Castes are still extremely rare. Ambedkar himself married a Brahmin woman late in his life, and some people I met were able to cite an instance or two that they knew personally, but these were all cases in which concealment was not being attempted. One man said:

Just yesterday a Scheduled Caste boy married a Sonar girl, a caste Hindu, though both families objected. He is a clerk in my office. The girl is better off and better educated than he is. They met in a night school where they formed a friendship. I too objected and tried to dissuade him from it. These marriages do not work out successfully. I know a Scheduled Caste man married to a Brahmin girl, but she is not at home in his family environment and every day their life gets worse. In the joint family, it is almost impossible. When a couple lives alone it is a little easier.

[34] Cf., C. T. Kannan, *Intercaste and Intercommunity Marriages in India*, Bombay, 1963.

The point about marriage is that ex-Untouchables who pass are unlikely to find mates for their children outside their caste, and if they do, they are unlikely to be able to keep their own caste background hidden. "It is possible, but not very likely," said one informant. "In India everybody knows everybody's caste one way or another, sooner or later. The educated people can separate, yet they can't separate, for community is part of this society. You can't be without a community. Without a community, it is awkward for a man in all his relationships. This is the culture of the country. *In India you have got to be connected.*"

The inescapable facts of caste life in India have led some ex-Untouchables to devise an in-between style, a kind of semi-passing, as the solution to their problems. Put a bit roughly, it is a system for passing in public while not passing in private. In general it means that in all situations where self-advancement, comfort, and convenience dictate it, an ex-Untouchable passes as a member of some higher caste. At the same time, in all the circumstances that demand it—death, marriage, even voluntary work for the community—he leads a second or double life in the bosom of his community. I met several individuals who were trying to organize their lives this way and they did their best to explain to me just how they managed it. The technique is to take a name that might be common to more than one upper caste, so that by name alone, it might be assumed by people that you belong to any one of the possible castes it suggests. You are prepared if necessary to claim one of these castes as your own, but generally speaking, the appearance of things is hopefully enough for most purposes. As one of these individuals explained: "The idea is that you adopt the appearance of being of a higher caste through your name and your way of life.

Your professional associates must not know about you in too much detail. You can have your social life with them, but you avoid having this social life grow too close. You go to tea, but you avoid having dinner, that's too close, and you avoid that." And why not dinner? I asked. "Well, when you take dinner," came the answer, "you take it in a particular manner. You might eat out of the pot, or do something that is not right and spoil the whole relation. At the same time," he went on, "you keep your connection with your community in all such things as arranging marriages, family affairs, observing ceremonies. Thus in your public and professional life you appear to be of another caste while in your private, personal life, you are of your own community. This is difficult, but it is not so difficult as trying to disappear away from the community altogether."

It takes strong nerves to live in this fashion but it can evidently be done. My informant illustrated how it worked in one crisis that had occurred not very long before in his own life. "One of my relatives who was living with me died at the hospital," he said. "I should have taken her body to my own house, but I took her to my brother's house in the community in order to avoid any embarrassment with others where I lived. Any ceremony that might reveal to others we are of Scheduled Caste, we hold in a relative's home."

Among those I met who are engaged in this tightrope operation as a way of life was a lawyer who told me he had taken his name, a common upper caste name, while he was still in law school. He went through the proper legal procedure, a formal application, publication in the gazette, and so on. It took two months. His diploma was made out in his new name, "and in this way," he said, "I started out fresh." Thanks to a "certain fraternity" of people engaged in this way of life, he was able to get started on his practice, intimating that some friends who knew who he was sent him some clients for a start.

I get caste Hindu clients, Mohammedan clients, and a few Scheduled Caste people who know me. About 90 percent of my clients do not know I belong to the Scheduled Castes. If they knew, they would not employ me, so naturally I have to conceal it. It is a problem. In the profession, people generally do not know I am Scheduled Caste, though some of my associates and a few lawyers do know. I mix with many non-Scheduled Caste advocates at dinner, lunch, tea, sometimes I even go to their homes. My wife—who is Scheduled Caste and is educated up to matric—does not go with me on such occasions. It is not the custom. They come to my home too, perhaps two or three times a year. I live in a neighborhood where all high caste people live. They do not know there that we are Scheduled Caste. I have some good friends whom I visit often, perhaps every week or so. Some of them know what I am, some do not.

He was able, it seemed, to keep a mental card file and always to know who knew what he was and who did not know. If this was a wearing business, he gave no sign of it. Indeed, it was when individuals were talking to me about things like this that I felt least sure that I had any idea how they actually *felt* about what they were telling me. I had to assume that on this subject, above all, they were guarding themselves psychologically as well as they could. There were confusions and contradictions and unclarities when we got down to details, but I had to be content with leaving most of them unexplored. This was especially true when I asked the most troubling question of all: What about the children, what do you tell your children?

11. *TELLING THE CHILDREN*

Whenever the subject of children came up in my talks with educated ex-Untouchables, things invariably began to get very confused. What had been up to that point a reasonably clear line of communication suddenly became clogged. Facts would get unclear or contradictory, or so at least they would seem to me. I was handicapped here by considerable ignorance. I do not know what life is like in these families or how parents and children communicate with each other. A father might say to me: "My son [or daughter] does not know about Untouchability." Sometimes this turned out to mean that he was saying that his child had not actually experienced Untouchability in its more traditional forms. But then he might also say: "He [or she] does not know we come of an Untouchable community." Even the most tentative pursuit of this statement would quickly show that the child, no longer an infant and often already an adolescent or not far from it, would have to be deaf, dumb, and blind not to know a great deal more about himself and his family than the father either would or could acknowledge. A father would frequently say that his child did not know any of this because the child had never asked and he, the father, had never told. When I would ask whether the child did not learn these things outside the home, from schoolmates or neighborhood children, I would sometimes get a blank stare, or a blank denial, or: "No, the matter has never come up." And this might be followed a few minutes later by details that showed that it had indeed

come up in one way or another. What every one of these
men wanted more than anything else was to blot out the
legacy of the past and to give his children a new identity of
their own. They seemed to feel that awareness of the past
status was enough to instill "feelings of inferiority." In their
own families and with their own children, they tried to deal
with this problem by simply not talking about it. I never
felt free to push too far into the confusions that always sur-
rounded this question. This was the most sensitive ground
I found myself on in all my encounters with educated ex-
Untouchables, and I trod upon it softly.

In the case of one young man, still unmarried at thirty-
four, the characteristic cloud of denial and/or confusion had
settled in his own mind over his own childhood. His father
was a motor mechanic and they lived in "two good rooms"
in government quarters in Bombay. His father never told
him anything about this, he said, and it was not until he got
his leaving certificate at the end of the 4th standard when he
was ten that he learned that he was "Mahar." But even this
had no meaning to him, he said. "I did not take it to mean
anything." He said he had never had any reason to think of
himself as "Hindu" either. "I never heard of Scheduled
Castes," he continued in this remarkable catalogue of non-
awareness, "until I filled out the form for my first year at
college. I had never heard of it before. That was in 1953."
But a few minutes later he was telling me how his father
was a follower of Ambedkar, how the whole family had gone
to meetings, and how as a small boy he had heard of the
Scheduled Castes Federation, though, he added, "I didn't
know the meaning of it."

This was a rather extreme case, but it illustrated some of
the complications involved in this matter. Several men with
young children told me that they had never told their children anything about their background, and expressed the

belief that their children knew nothing about it. But then they would go on to tell me how they had taken their youngsters back to their family villages for visits and I was left to wonder what they thought their children learned there. I met one father who emphatically declared he would never take his children back to the village for this very reason. "My son is fourteen," said this senior civil servant in Bangalore, "and I have never taken him back to the village. I don't want my children to have any experience of Untouchability. They don't know what it is, they have never experienced it. I don't think they are clear about what it is, even though they have read about it in books. They do not identify themselves with it. My son goes to public school in a mixed class and it does not come up. He knows he is Adikarnataka, but he does not know his identity as an Untouchable."

My Congress M.P. acquaintance in New Delhi first said: "Up to now I have not told my children. I have sons twelve, ten, and nine, and a daughter, five. I have not told them all the things that have happened." But then he added: "Now my oldest son knows that he belongs to such a caste, though up to a year ago I avoided it. He asked me one day: 'Father, what caste do we belong to—the boys were saying that you are a Chamar—is this correct?' I said, 'Yes, this is correct.' But up to that time none of the children had known about these things. Now they understood that they belong to a lower caste, much lower than the others. Here in Delhi they feel no effect of it, they go to school here." Then, as if to complete the confusions in his account, he went on: "We get back to our village once a year. They still feel it there, living separately, not allowed into houses, and so on." His sons came in to be introduced and they shyly received some of my questions. The small boy said in English: "I want to be a leader." What kind of leader? I asked. He looked up at his father and said: "I want to be a Member of Parliament."

In Bombay a short, sharp-featured young man who aspires to become a professor of law was quite certain he was going to be able to start his children out quite fresh.

They won't know what the Scheduled Caste is. They will live in an advanced way. I now live among Catholics and Anglo-Indians. I will tell my daughter she is Buddhist. Why should I tell her about our community? I won't have to. It will just be forgotten. When my daughter grows up we will just be Buddhists.

A well-placed civil servant who lives in a caste Hindu neighborhood took me somewhat further into this business of what the children know.

My daughter (who is eleven) does not know she is Dhor. She has seen the tanning business in Dharabi, the section of Bombay where all the tanners, the Dhors and the Chamars live. We lived there until 1960 when we moved to a better place. She never asked. The question never arose. Most of the people there are Dhors, so they don't ask. When we moved, nobody questioned us. She has never asked. People elsewhere, as in Poona or Kholapur, still ask what community you belong to, and the children become conscious of it. If my children ever ask me, I'll tell them the truth. My brothers and sisters, who stay with me in the same house, they know, but my children do not. Yes, it is a joint household, but the question never does come up. The children have gone to marriages but they are not conscious of caste or community. They don't know that Untouchability exists. My young sister and brother do know, but my daughter does not. She will come to know it gradually. This is just striking me now, because you are asking me. I never had an idea about it. Most parents will avoid this discussion with their younger children because they think it will have an effect on their minds. They don't want their children to have a complex that we are lower and other people higher. We want our children to think that everybody is equal. I will have to explain to my children that when I was a child, I stood at the door of the classroom with the

Scheduled Castes, that nobody mixed with us, but that I was first in the class. I will explain the history and my experience so that they won't feel inferior, that we should not feel inferior to any community in India. There *is* a stigma in belonging to the Scheduled Castes. Other people will think a Scheduled Caste person is inferior, and the other person's behavior changes when he finds out, like my superior when he learned I was Scheduled Caste. He was surprised I could come to such a position. As my daughter grows up, she must learn about our community, but she must have no complexes about it.

A school administrator began by giving me the familiar assurance his son "does not know he belongs to an Untouchable caste." He knows that their community was "Mahar" and that they are now "Buddhist," but he knows nothing at all about Untouchability. "We take care that no inferiority complex should seep into his mind. Most people might not be so careful and their children might be able to tell that they belong to an Untouchable caste." But he was quite sure that his eleven-year-old son did not know.

His boy, he then went on to tell me, goes to a private primary school run by caste Hindus—Brahmins, in fact—under the name Aryan Education Society. As I took in this almost indigestibly ironic bit of information, he was adding: "They know there he is a Scheduled Caste boy. There are only two Scheduled Caste boys in the school." I asked whether the other boys knew his son was Scheduled Caste. "I don't know," he answered. "Usually they don't inquire." What happened when there were fights or arguments, I wanted to know. He said he had not heard of any from his son. "He will learn of his past from *us*," he offered and then continued, as if in a dialogue with himself:

But why should he learn it? He will only say he is Buddhist. This will tell others that he is former Scheduled Caste and this means they might see him from a special point of view, for they will understand he comes from the Mahar community. But those brought up on Ambedkar's teachings know about Untouchability and will reject the inferiority coming from it. Others called us inferior, but *we* do not see ourselves as inferior, now or in the past.

He went on to repeat the Mahar-Buddhist view of the inherent inequality of Hinduism and how emancipation was achieved by leaving Hinduism altogether and becoming Buddhists. "Why not explain all this to your son?" I asked. "This is not the age to do so," he answered. "He might get a complex from the fact that his fathers were inferior. The development of his mind must come first." And when would that come? I asked. "He must gradually come to know," he insisted, ignoring my question. But when would he be ready? I insisted. He paused. Then unexpectedly he said: "You know the capacity of Indian boys to understand this kind of thing is different from boys of advanced countries." I asked: "Suppose your son gets into an argument with some caste Hindu boys and he learns that way?" He looked at me for a moment. "I don't know, I never thought about this question." I waited, and then he cried out with some anger. "But I don't see *why* we should tell our boys they belonged to such a caste!" Could it be concealed? "I do not want to conceal it!" he answered heatedly. "But if I tell him, he will get a sort of inferiority complex. He knows Mahar, but he does not know about Untouchability. If he comes to know at a later stage, the knowledge won't affect him." Then he said, weakly, suddenly folding: "It is our problem. We are not sure ourselves when to tell our boys." He fell silent, and then: "I am not able to answer this question. I am not able to know."

My acquaintance from Kerala told me that when his children were small they went back to his native Trivandrum

and discovered there that they belonged to "a very low
community." Since they had been raised in New Delhi where
their father was a political figure, "they simply refused to
accept it." But his youngest son was put in school there, and
this was what happened then:

He was given a very high standing because of his background
in the New Delhi public school. He entered Standard 6. The
teacher asked how many Scheduled Caste children there were
and told them to stand up. My son was nine years old. He didn't
know he was Scheduled Caste. We had never spoken of being
Paravan or anything like that. The teacher called to him and
said: "You are getting a scholarship. You are Scheduled Caste,
so stand up!" The teacher was a caste Hindu. My son stood up.
"Which community do you belong to?" the teacher asked. My
son did not know so he did not answer. He came home and
asked me what group we belonged to. "The teacher said I was
Scheduled Caste," he said. "Is that correct?" And I said, yes,
that's correct, you belong to the Scheduled Caste. He said: "I
stood up and I was the only Scheduled Caste student in the
class." My wife and I laughed, making a joke of it. He felt a
little solitary, lonely. I could not realize the intensity of it. I
don't think he realized too much about it; at least from his face
and expression, he did not seem too unhappy about it. "Then
what caste do I belong to?" he asked. "I couldn't say anything
in the class!" I said I belonged to Paravan and his mother belonged to the Pulayan caste, and that finished the conversation.
In all this, the question of Untouchability did not come up.
We did not tell him about it. The other children did not say
anything about it either, as far as I know. He did not ask and we
did not tell him. To this day he does not know that he came
from an Untouchable caste, and my daughter does not know
either. He is in a Christian missionary school, an Anglican
school for Anglo-Indians. There aren't many there who aren't
Anglo-Indians. I want him to grow up out of his caste, not with
Hindus. In Trivandrum he had too much of this and that's why

I thought going to the south was a very bad idea. Our children are without caste. They know they are Hindus, but are without caste.

For people who are "passing," it all gets even more complicated because they have to draw their children into their conspiracies of concealment. A man of the Mahayanshi community of Gujarat told me he has two baby sons, still too young for these confusions, but he also has a daughter of thirteen. His story:

She knows she belongs to the Mahayanshi community. She heard this word long ago but had no concept of what it meant until one time five years ago when we took her to our family village for a visit. It was the first time she had ever been there. We had to stay in our separate place. The other children asked her who she was and she said she was my daughter, and they said: "Oh, then you are Mahayanshi, as we are." She was very offended. They were very poor children and she learned she was in their caste. She could not go into any home in the village, or shop. She had to stand outside. That was in our village, only five years ago, 156 miles from Bombay.

My wife was brought up in Poona in a cosmopolitan atmosphere. She came to our village when we were married. I was twenty-two then and she was eighteen and she learned of the village conditions that time. She had the same disappointing things happen to her when we came to visit my family. But she did not tell our daughter about it. She thought things might have improved. Now my daughter is in 7th standard. At school she gives the name of a Gujarat caste, which is what we tell people who ask us, for if we disclosed our true caste people would frown on us and not give us respect. She knows that if she said she was Mahayanshi, there would be some sort of dislike toward her. Now people look on her with regard and affection. They would not do so if they knew she was Scheduled Caste. She is telling a lie, but it is not difficult. It is not a good idea, telling lies, but it is not difficult. In Bombay we live among non-

Scheduled Caste people. The moment I disclosed that I was Scheduled Caste, there would be some sort of non-cooperation. They would try to harass us until we left the place.

I asked how his daughter felt about all of this. He shrugged. "She's not worried now about the future. My daughter will be married in our community. Others will be bound to know one day. Some friends will continue their friendship with her, some will not, and those that keep on being friends, it will be a shallow friendship. In my own case, I feel that I will not be mindful what other people do. She will be mature enough also later on and will decide what to do." I asked if there was any chance that she might marry outside her community. "I think not," her father answered. "No one will be ready for that." Does she talk about this with her friends? "I don't think so," he said. I explained that I meant Mahayanshi friends. "Oh no," he replied, "there aren't any Mahayanshi in the vicinity. She has no such friends. At school things will just go on. School friendships come to an end. Very few continue. Then she will go on to high school and make new friends. When I have to fill out the form for college, I will say she is Scheduled Caste to get the rights and facilities. As far as her student friends are concerned, she won't disclose our caste. If they come to know, yes, for example, from the notice of scholarships, well, all right, they will come to know!" He did not seem to think this would present much of a problem and when I asked whether he thought his daughter would be unhappy over it, he shrugged again. "Not necessarily," he said. "If the others take it in good spirit, it will make no difference. If they look at it with prejudice, then there will be some difficulty, because the prejudices are that we are ignorant people, with no ability. My own idea is that if people come to know I am Mahayanshi, I will not bother about it. They can adopt any course they like as far as I am concerned, but on my own account, I will not tell anybody I am of Scheduled Caste. This is how I hope it will be with my daughter."

When she got married, he went on, she would marry someone of their own caste, but at the wedding none of her friends would discover the bridegroom's caste. "Mahayanshis are married by Hindu rites," he explained, "and there is no clue to caste just by looking at the ceremony; you can't tell. There will be other non-Scheduled Caste guests and no one will discover anything about our caste. The priest may be under the impression that we are of some higher caste, he would not know. If he did know we were Scheduled Caste, it would probably make no difference if he agreed to come in the first place. The ceremony would not be any different. If he did not agree to come, I would get another priest who would."

All this was said in a vigorous, confident way. He gave the air of knowing just what he was about and having it all taped down well into the future. I wondered whether he really did or whether he was fooling himself, and I subsequently put the question to a number of others: would it be possible to have a wedding ceremony and reception without the guests learning the caste of the principals? Other Scheduled Caste people looked at me incredulously when I put the question. "Impossible!" came the reply again and again. "Why, the guests talk with each other, somebody is going to ask where the family comes from, there is always some curious person, and one way or another the name of the community will come out." Or again: "Even if they don't talk, the caste Hindu guests will be able to tell from the speech and dress of the relatives, because if there are relatives they are surely poorer relatives and you can always tell." It was suggested that if the host invited only those members of his family who were also prosperous and could dress and talk well, he might just get away with it, barring that one curious guest who might ferret out the truth anyway. Against all this there was the testimony of one Parsi lady I asked who described her wedding-going experiences in a way that suggested that if this man chose his guests with care he might indeed carry it off just as he said he could. "Why, of course I never learn the caste of the people," said the Parsi lady. "I have often been invited to weddings in the families of associates at the university. I go and sit down and I'm quiet. I don't really know anybody there. All the other people talk some, but mostly they also just sit down. The ceremony takes about an hour. Then I go up and express my good wishes to the family, and I leave. I might not say more than a few sentences to anybody the whole time and I would certainly never know anything about their caste!" It is also possible, of course, that being a Parsi and not a Hindu, the question of their caste would be less likely to enter her mind.

Getting back to my original informant on this matter, besides the daughter who would figure in this problematic wedding, he had two small sons and I asked him what he thought about the outlook for their future. "We will see what development there will be in the society by 1970 and 1980," he calmly replied, and then went on:

If caste prejudice is wiped away, then no difficulty. If it is still here, then we will follow our practice. We will remain Mahayanshi in private and our higher caste in public. If there is no prejudice or hatred, then there will be no more problem about coming out with it. If there is no distinction between treatment of Brahmin and Scheduled Caste, then fine. If all caste is abolished, that will be fine too. But I think the problems will remain. It is all not likely to change too much. The caste system will remain and we will find ways to deal with it, to show we are in no way inferior. Different people will give various caste names to hide their original caste. We can do this for years, and it may just go on and on.

12. WAYS OUT

In the minds of the ex-Untouchables I met, the future took
on many different shades and shapes. I did not meet any
who were bouncing with bright optimism but neither was
anyone plunged into bleak despair. The older ones were
weary and rather discouraged. Among the younger ones,
there were rising expectations, each one for himself and his
own prospects more than for the larger group. I certainly
do not enlarge the small number of people I met to a sample
of statistical significance. Even less do I feel that I grasped
with any certainty the quality of the deeper and more inward
feelings of any of these individuals. That would take more
time, more knowing. Still, it seems to me rather extraordinary
that I came upon only one person who had been pushed by
all these circumstances into a condition of violent anger
openly expressed. This was a young man who rose in a meeting I had with a group of students in the city of Mysore, made
a long speech, and wound up with: "The Congress Party is
making fools of the Scheduled Castes! We need to revolt
against the whole caste system! Half of all the caste Hindus
must be killed, immediately! I can't tolerate it!"

Among the several dozen young people I interviewed,
there was one who told me he "hated" Brahmins. Another
burst out suddenly with: "I want to avenge my people! I want
to *do* something!" When I asked how he thought he could
avenge them, he answered deflatedly: "I can't say. I don't
know how. Oh, why do they hate us? Now we are educated.

There is the barbarous way, to fight, and that way I don't like. The second is the civilized way, to go ahead and be equal."

But most of those to whom I spoke did not express these feelings, even though one assumed they had to be there. There was the story of an older man who told me how he had won his way to higher education by reading his books under Bombay streetlamps and had finally been admitted to a college there in 1941.

After six months at the college, I started suffering from head-aches. Because of these headaches I was in inter-Arts [second year of the degree course] for three years. I suffered three failures because I couldn't work. I joined a government department as a clerk in 1943, working on reading for my exam and hoping that my headaches would just disappear, that I would be able to get through. I went to many doctors, but nobody could diagnose it. Big doctors operated twice inside my nose, but I was not cured. A brain specialist examined me and said he could do nothing. I tried a nature cure, according to Ayurvedic medicine, but I only managed to gain some weight. I had to pay what I could for all this medical service out of my salary of R90 ($18.90) a month and of course I could not save anything. Finally in 1944, I passed my inter-Arts exam and went on for my B.A. and got through the B.A. in 1947. I still get headaches.

I asked a psychiatrist in Bombay about this, a Muslim who had received his training in England. "All the feelings you *think* ought to be there *are* there," he said, "only they are very well repressed." He believed this to be the pattern among Indians generally who, he said, were even more given than other people to "make-believe" in dealing with life's problems. This remained at best a guess, for I gathered from him and others that very little still is known about the ef-fects of specific cultural patterns on the psychodynamics of

individuals, particularly in India where there are deep
blocks against this kind of analytical self-scrutiny.

But all the ex-Untouchables with whom I talked did share
one clear and common wish: to be freed of the stigma of
having been Untouchables. For this they had to cease also to
be ex-Untouchables. They had to become something different,
something no longer connected in any way to the rejected
past. What they wanted was wholly new identities for themselves that would be accepted in the society. This was, to be
sure, no small wish. To realize it for the great mass of ex-
Untouchables, the whole of Indian society will have to make
itself over, conquer its economic and social backwardness,
abolish caste, and put all of its people on some new common
footing. This is not something anyone in India expects to
come about soon. If there was any despair in the ex-Untouchable outlook as I found it, it was over the distance
and dimness of this prospect of large change. Still each man
meanwhile must shape his own view of the future he wants
for himself and, where he must, the group to which he finds
himself attached. Among those I talked to, I found four main
ideas about this, four ways out for the ex-Untouchable. The
first and main one was economic self-betterment. The second
was to get out of the caste system altogether by quitting
Hinduism and embracing another religion. The third was to
remain Hindu and inside the caste system but to achieve
true touchability for their castes. The last, the most flickering
of these hopes, was to have their new identities as *Indians*,
citizens of the new Indian nation, become strong enough to
replace, or at least to dominate, the caste or group identities
they might still continue to have.

Self-betterment in India has to begin with education, and
as far as the ex-Untouchables are concerned, this has so far
affected only 10 percent of their number. Only the young

people now in school can be counted on to acquire new outlooks, new wants, and to reach for new positions in the society. The great mass of millions of ex-Untouchables in their villages have had their status changed by legal fiat but hardly in any other way. They remain where they are caught in the great mess of backwardness, perhaps here and there becoming aware of new pressures and new possibilities, but seeing themselves nowhere in any new picture. This was not something I could undertake to explore [35] but I do carry with me a sharp memory of the time we cut in a mile or so from the highway in southern India, left the car, and walked on into a village, and through the village to the ramshackle huts of the Scheduled Caste quarter on its far side. A crowd quickly gathered around us in the sun, with the caste Hindu villagers standing apart at the outer edge, silently curious. Our host and guide, a young official from the Department of Welfare, put to them our wish to know what, if anything, was different in this village now from the way it was ten years back. The answers were that nothing was different, everything was the same. "But aren't your children going to school?" we asked. There were blank stares first, and then words, and our interpreter said: "They say yes, but that makes things different for their children, not for them."

Even the picture of quickening progress through ever-expanding education has to be qualified. In the villages there is still a profound inertia and a failure on a vast scale to take up the opportunities now offered to send children to school. Many thoughtful people were troubled, moreover, by a falling off of the momentum in the cities, an ebbing of the initial drive among the lower economic groups in the cities to get education both for themselves and their children. The "dropout" problem in Indian terms is the dropout at the 4th

[35] See Kusum Nair, *Blossoms in the Dust*, London, 1961, for one reporter's firsthand view of the state of affairs in India's villages.

standard, where great masses of ten- or eleven-year-old youngsters terminate their school careers and fall back into the
slums and the terrible ruts of their great common poverty
and backwardness.

But it is with those who stay on the educational path and
do move up that the hope of individual self-betterment does
burn brightly. Their dogged efforts are aimed at particular
goals, at jobs that are going to bring with them the rise in
income, the rise in place, the rise in social status—the heart
and core of the business of getting ahead in the world. As
for most of the 300,000 who already occupy such places,
this can be a very modest goal indeed, any such job represent-
ing enough of a rise in life to be a victory over one's past.
This is a gain of no small magnitude for the great hosts of
white-shirted clerks and petty officials, and even for many of
those who find regular and more dignified employment, at
the lowest levels, in government industries and enterprises.
For a much smaller number, higher goals beckon. "I want to
become I.A.S., a deputy commissioner, anywhere in India, and
maybe I'll be there in five years' time." Another: "If I pass
that [I.A.S.] examination, I'll be a civil servant until I retire.
If I don't pass in two years, I'll practice law and will join
politics—I don't know yet which party." Another sets his eye
beyond government on a private path to advancement: "I
want to become a Chartered Accountant. No Scheduled
Caste person ever has. I will make 800 rupees [$168] a
month!" Another, aiming to become a lawyer, tells me he
is not going to be deflected by politics but is going to work
hard at practicing his profession. "Then I want to come back
and become a professor of law at this college. I will get 600
rupees [$126] to begin with, 700 rupees [$147] if I get to be
an examiner."

The dream of the better life that goes with this advancement popped up here and there among these hopes for the future. One young man who is the son of a laborer and aspires to become an industrial chemist said:

My pleasures are to read novels in Marathi and English and detective books, like Agatha Christie and Erle Stanley Gardner. I like going to movies, social movies, fine subjects that give us good morals. There are no good movies about everyday life, only third-class persons wearing first-class clothes. . . .

An undergraduate whose father works for the telephone company and whose own ambition is to get a job in a private firm, said:

My wants in life are higher than my father's. He lived many years in the village. I have lived my life in the city. I like to go to film shows. He never liked this. My father did not want to go to a hotel to take a meal, but I do. I do go to a hotel for a meal, and I like better clothes.

The idea of the magic of *better clothes* as an escape from ex-Untouchability recurred more than once, never more vividly than in the story of the son of a well-placed politician who was able to have money in his pocket when he went to the university. He came out of his time there with his own quite clear idea of what it took to get ahead in the world. His father being a Congress notable, he was, incidentally, one of the very few ex-Untouchables I met in India who made free use of the term "Harijan" as he talked.

I think show is important in society, dress, money. If you are well dressed and have money, nobody will bother you. It is only assumed you are very high, a Brahmin or a Reddy [another high caste in his home province]. The main thing to come up with is money and education. If a person has these two things, nobody can point a finger at him as a Harijan. You can be bold in talking, if you have money and clothes.

This young man had traveled with a well-to-do caste Hindu crowd at the campus and evidently had become very much one of the group. Then came the day when his name appeared on the scholarship list.

People refused to believe it. The list on the notice board came as a big shock to all my friends. "What is this?" they asked. "Your name on the list?" Another said, "What did you do, bluff the authorities into believing you are Harijan so you could get a scholarship?" You see, the Mala has an inferiority complex. Nobody expects him to be a well-placed man in society. So they just couldn't believe it. People would ask me to swear that I was really Harijan and when I swore, they would be shocked all the more.

I asked him how this made him feel. He looked surprised at the question.

I used to be proud at people not thinking I was Harijan. I felt they were respecting me and not seeing me as Harijan when I did not appear to be Harijan. In this way I was happy, but I guess I was sad a little bit too, all people thinking I was not Harijan. My conscience pricked at telling a lie. [It was not clear what lie he had been telling, but his well-to-do caste Hindu friends obviously had him otherwise identified until that list appeared on the bulletin board!] It was not a shame to be born in a Harijan family. I should not feel bad about it. But that all those others should know that I was Harijan made me feel proud, proud that I could defeat them in *their* ideas about what a Harijan was. I used to see how they would treat the other Harijan students who were ill-dressed and didn't have enough pocket money or books. The other Harijans would look at me with respect that I could move so freely with the caste Hindus. The Harijans did not move with me. Very few of the caste Hindus knew I was Harijan. I was happy to have the good chance to get their respect. The Harijan boys had a complex about themselves, but I did not.

He was now in a government job but he wanted to get out into private business.

I don't want to stick to a government job but to get into business, anything that will be better paid. Of course, one's position is not as safe in business as in the government. In government, once you join it, it's hard to get you out. In business you can be removed, but there is more pay. I want to float a business of my own and have an income or perhaps R3,000 or R5,000 [$630 to $1,050] a month, with a bungalow of my own, a palatial house of my own, and some cars.

It was this young man's brother, quoted earlier, whose sights were set higher and who said confidently, "I'm going to be a millionaire."

Emergence from poverty would of course provide an ultimate answer to many problems for the ex-Untouchables along with the rest of India's poverty-held masses. A few ex-Untouchables may share in the rise of the new Indian middle class but it will be a long time before they become numerous enough to reflect a change in the status of ex-Untouchables generally. In any case, even given the best of all possible outcomes in India's struggle for economic advancement during the coming decades—and optimism in this respect has to be restrained—it remains clear that the rising ex-Untouchable's problems will not be met by rupees alone. The society will be wrestling for generations to come with what one Hindu liberal has called "the monster of caste." So will the ex-Untouchable. Meanwhile, he will have to cope with all the burdens it imposes upon him. One way some have taken has been to quit the Hindu fold altogether, to escape caste by leaving the religion that supports it. This is the way out through conversion.

Over time great numbers of Untouchables have abandoned Hinduism to seek greater dignity for themselves in the holding of other beliefs. At various periods of this long history, they have become Buddhists, Muslims, and Christians. B. R. Ambedkar foreshadowed his own move in this direction quite early in his career. In a famous speech in 1936 he put an Untouchable declaration of independence from Hinduism on the same footing as a Hindu declaration of independence from Britain. "Just as Swaraj [self-rule] is necessary for India," he said, "so also is a change of religion necessary for the Untouchables. The underlying motive in both movements is the desire for freedom." He went on:

My self-respect cannot assimilate Hinduism.... I tell you, religion is for man, not man for religion. If you want to organize, consolidate, and be successful in this world, change this religion. The religion that does not recognize you as human beings, or give you water to drink, or allow you to enter the temples is not worthy to be called a religion.... The religion that does not teach its followers to show humanity in dealing with its co-religionists is nothing but a display of force. The religion that asks its adherents to suffer the touch of animals but not the touch of human beings is not a religion but a mockery. The religion that compels the ignorant to be ignorant and the poor to be poor is not religion but a visitation! [36]

Not until 20 years later, after much wrestling with the Hindus and much painful contemplation of alternatives, did Ambedkar finally choose Buddhism as the way out for the Untouchables because it rejected caste and in matters of the soul offered equal status to all men. Another reason was that it was close enough to the tradition of the culture not to "denationalize" those who embraced it. Buddha, after all, was a Hindu himself, whose appeal to the common humanity of all men 2,500 years ago brought him into conflict with the Hindu powers of his day. One view is that

36 Keer, pp. 273–4.

Buddhism was never able to establish itself successfully in the land of its birth because it threatened the social structure maintained by the Hindus, and it is one of Ambedkar's theories that the first Untouchables were those who were punished in this way for embracing the radical doctrine. Eventually, Buddha was taken in as a Hindu deity and his doctrines successfully Hinduized. On this, again, there is much obscurity and controversy. The relevant point is that Ambedkar chose Buddhism not only for what he felt it preached, but because it too was native to his native land. He had over the years given thought to Sikhism, a younger, 500-year-old offshoot of Hinduism, and Islam and Christianity, both of which came to India more than 1,000 years ago. Even after partition and the transfer of most of India's Muslims to the sovereignty of Pakistan, India still retained a Muslim minority of 45,000,000 people. Indian Christians number some 10,000,000, more than half of them Roman Catholics. There are Nestorian Christian communities in Malabar that date back to sometime in the 5th century A.D., and tradition dates a first arrival to St. Thomas' coming in 52 A.D. The Portuguese brought Roman Catholicism to the country in the sixteenth century, and the British Protestants came a century later. Both Islam and Christianity attracted large numbers of Untouchables, though no one now could say how many. There is a record of Christian effort for the uplift of these lowly castes. There is also a remarkable record of Hindu caste lines being carried over and maintained within the social systems of both the Christians and the Muslims. This arresting fact came to more general attention only in more recent years in a peculiarly ironic way when the advantages for ex-Untouchables in the form of government benefits began to outweigh the feeling of stigma attached to Untouchability. Christian Untouchables, Sikh Untouchables, and apparently also Muslim Untouchables began clamoring to be counted in. Caste Hindus have not always been able to avoid a certain malice in their references to this rather striking fact. Here, for example, is what K. Kalelkar, then chairman of the government's Backward Classes Commission, had to say about this in 1955:

The Muslims and the Christians had always prided themselves on being free from caste. But ever since the moment the Swaraj government gave liberal concessions to the Scheduled Castes and the backward people, both Muslims and Christians have been enthusiastically trying to prove that there is caste and Untouchability in their midst, and the Christians have successfully proved that caste Christians looked down on Harijan Christians and kept them aloof both in life and in death. The Harijan Christians in some regions were kept outside the church for a long time. Then they were allowed to sit in the church in a separate wing. Even today Christians belonging to Untouchable castes are forced to have separate cemeteries in some parts of India. Even the dead must observe caste and Untouchability! ... Muslims have told me that they generally do not tolerate marriages between higher caste Muslims and the scavenging Muslims or butcher Muslims....[37]

He no doubt had good political reasons for not adding similar remarks about the Sikhs, for whom special exceptions had to be made in a government ruling excluding all non-Hindus from these benefits. The rule, handed down in 1950, stated: "No person who professes a religion different from Hinduism shall be deemed to be a member of the Scheduled Castes." This caused years of agitation, court cases, rulings, and counter-rulings, with different regulations coming into effect in different states. In the end the non-Hindu ex-Untouchables emerged with some share in the special privileges of the Scheduled Castes but by no means what they felt to be an equal share. As one report recently put it: "There are still

[37] *Report of Seminar on Casteism*, pp. 50–51.

very few states where it is as advantageous economically to be a Christian or a Buddhist of Harijan background as it is to be a Hindu Harijan." [38]

Earlier in these pages my informant from Kerala described his experience at a Catholic school which was operated, as far as Untouchables were concerned, just like a caste Hindu institution, with separation and exclusion as commonly practiced by caste Hindus. He also told me the story of his wife's family which lived in the neighboring state of Cochin. Her father and a whole group had been converted by an Anglican priest some time around 1910. "There were about fifty Pulaya families who had become Anglican but when they came to the church, they were made to stay in a separate corner," he said. "So my wife's father said never mind, they would build their own church. And this they did, and an Indian Anglican father would come over and give them communion separately so that the caste Anglicans and the Untouchable Anglicans were kept apart." A Gujarati told me that a group of people in a village of his district became Christians.

When they have to approach any official bureau for anything, they say they are Scheduled Caste. But if you approach them privately, they will tell you they are Christian. They became Catholics. They don't have a church but they put up a picture of Christ. There is a priest in a village a mile away. He is a land cultivator who also preaches. He does not say mass. These people say they are Christian as a kind of very mild protest. They are still treated exactly as they were before, no change at all, only a little more satisfaction among themselves.

The Mahars who followed Ambedkar are the only ex-Untouchables in India who have attempted to take the course of mass conversion as a way out of their sea of troubles. I was

38 Smith, *India as a Secular State*, p. 188.

told that as many as two and a half million, or about half the total Mahar population, have embraced Buddhism. How accurate this may be and what it means to "embrace Buddhism," I could not say. These converts are often called "Neo-Buddhists" and will demand that they be called "just Buddhists," but whether Neo-Buddhists or Buddhists, the new label remains for all practical purposes synonymous with "Mahar" which in turn automatically evokes "Untouchable." There is, finally, the added difficulty that to receive benefits they cannot declare themselves to be Buddhists but must, for official purposes, remain "Scheduled Caste." Again, I cannot say how far this has diluted the positive substance of the change. As my many interviews with Mahars have shown, however, the change in nominal identity has not been helpful up to this point in providing a change of identity in fact, and I am not at all sure how it has served individuals within themselves as a source of self-respect. Let me cite examples of three views. One is the unreserved acceptance:

No wise man wants to continue as a low caste man. Ambedkar embraced Buddhism and I went along with him. It is not easy to change religion so quickly, but Buddhism is really Hinduism minus the caste system. When I became a Buddhist in 1957, it changed my whole way of thinking. It made me feel I must go out and compete, that my children must get the highest kind of education, and enter into competition with all the general classes of the society.

A second convert feels less transformed:

Accepting a new religion won't help us in any economic or social way. Becoming "Buddhist" did not help. Now it is very difficult for me to say whether I am Hindu or Buddhist. It is not an easy job to follow Buddhism in the pure sense. I know, I am a student of history. Only highly intellectual persons can follow this religion. It is very difficult to follow. If you call yourself

Mahar, you belong to the Hindu religion and Hinduism is a religion based on inequality. Wherever there is Hinduism, democracy will not grow. Buddhism stands for equality and will help establish democracy in this country. So to a certain extent, I say I follow Buddhism.

A third younger man had no answer to the problem but he wanted no part of these hesitations.

I am not a Buddhist. I think changing name or religion won't remove these things. By converting to Buddhism you just change the name of the old Scheduled Castes. You have to change totally, not just the name, but totally, in thoughts, behavior, discipline of life, and everybody must change, not just the Scheduled Castes. If Buddhism were accepted by all, maybe there would be some sense in it. But if only one group does it, it just produces a new name. Persons who are converted, if asked what they are, say they are Buddhists. But they know they are Mahars, and the feeling is just the same. When I am asked—I don't feel ashamed of being a Mahar, but if I think it is asked with bad intentions, I say: "I am a human being." This is what I say. I hope my children will not experience any of this. I hope this question—who are you?— won't be asked. I hope my son will be not a Mahar, that he will be a man.

Many more ex-Untouchables want not to leave the Hindu fold but to achieve touchability inside of it. "Let each one remain in his caste, but let every caste be touchable." Variations of this formula appeared frequently in the talk of ex-Untouchables who were not followers of Ambedkar, who never dreamed of being anything but Hindus, who wanted to live in caste groups as they always had, but only to cease being pariahs, to become touchables.

Speaking of those who had moved into lower-level white collar jobs or into some non-menial industrial occupation or trade, a Mahayanshi in Bombay said:

Most of these people don't care about these problems. They live in a narrow circle and in this circle they don't have to care about Untouchability. But what they want generally would be to do away with Untouchability and retain the group, the caste. A few of the better-educated ones would want to get away from the group altogether but most of them would prefer to get away from being Untouchable while retaining the community, just to become touchable. This is what I think it would be right to say, that what we want is our caste, minus the Untouchability. I don't think anybody is against *all* caste!

More strongly positive about this was the young Dhor woman who had become a physician. She said:

God has created us in this community and we are proud. I want to see our community come up to a higher level, to the standard of the others. It shall remain a caste, but will become like the others. We were born in it, raised in it. Some may not like it because it is Scheduled Caste, but that does not mean that we should not like it. At present, marriage should stay within the caste. In the future if conditions change, it may not matter, but I would want my children to marry in the caste. We will tell our children that they are of our community. We will explain so that they will understand and know and help our community. We need more education, a better financial position, better treatment by higher caste people. It won't help just to change caste. It will need educated people to help others. I think this system of Untouchability will come to an end. It will take a long time, but it will come to an end.

This was essentially Gandhi's view of the way out: to preserve the caste system but to reform it by doing away with Untouchability, to give the Untouchables access to the temples, access to the common utilities such as wells, and assistance to raise their conditions of life to some more tolerable level, such as getting the night soil off their heads and into wheelbarrows. What Gandhi evidently wanted was not to abolish

caste as such but to restore the ancient system under which
there were only four large groups.[39] Although the post-
Gandhian Congress leadership has been ritually committed
to the more radical idea of abolishing caste altogether, its ac-
tions have conformed much more to an acceptance of the idea
that caste is here to stay, and the thing to do is to make it more
tolerable for the groups at the very bottom. What has been
legally "abolished" is not caste but Untouchability and the
problem is to transform this legal fact into social reality. Let
the Untouchable groups cross that line and rejoin the mass of
lowly Shudras, let them remain as humble as they might be,
let them retain all their divisions and subdivisions like
everyone else, but let them be *touchable*. This seemed, at any
rate, to be the ultimate hope of those I spoke to who were
not Mahars in Maharashtra but of other castes, like the
Dhors, or Chamars from Uttar Pradesh and the Punjab, the
Adikarnatakas and Chalavadis from Mysore, the Mahayanshis
from Gujarat, the Adi-Andhras and Malas from Andhra, and
the scattering of others I met—the Paravan, the Vankar, and
the rest. To be what they were, but to be relieved of the
degrading status they could no longer accept—this was the
hope, the prayer. But it was hardly the expectation. One
person said he thought it would take 100 years to accomplish,
another said 400.

There is a certain precedent for this in the Hindu system.
Despite its rigidities, some castes have been able to move
within it from one status to another. As it happened in the
past, this was a long, slow process that took generations. M. N.
Srinivas, the Indian anthropologist, has called this process
"Sanskritization," because a lower caste would begin to make
its way up by taking on the Sanskrit ritual of the Brahmins,
along with the higher caste practices of vegetarianism and

39 Cf. Ghurye, *Caste and Race in India*, pp. 182–83.

teetotalism. Starting with some economic, educational, or political improvement that gave them leverage, some members of a lower caste would break away and begin adopting the behavior patterns, ceremonies, habits, customs, and language style of the higher caste. It could take a long time, but eventually they would win recognition and acceptance at the higher rung of status. But, according to Srinivas, this kind of mobility took place only within the four large caste groups. It did not work for Untouchables who were "unable to cross the barrier of Untouchability ... the Untouchable caste is always forced to remain Untouchable." [40] It was theoretically possible for a group to cross that barrier only if it picked itself up bodily and moved to some distant area where nothing was known about it, something quite difficult to do in pre-British India and not much easier in British or, for that matter in post-British India. In recent years the new legal position, migration, urbanization, and modernization have introduced some new elements into the situation, and so have the politics of independent India where caste groups bargain with each other, a process that sometimes involves granting recognition of higher status to some caste group. Srinivas gives one example of this in Uttar Pradesh "where the Rajputs, who were until recently an exclusive group, seem to be more willing nowadays to grant Rajput status to aspiring groups with a view to strengthening themselves at the next elections." [41] In this case, the Rajputs were apparently trying to strengthen themselves against the Chamars, the major Untouchable group in the province, who were flirting with the Muslims and were therefore holding out social status-carrots to some of the lower touchable castes. In time, the ex-Un-

40 Cf., M. N. Srinivas, "A Note on Sanskritization and Westernization," *Far Eastern Quarterly*, v. XV, August 1956, pp. 481–496.

41 M. N. Srinivas, "Caste In India," *Journal of Asian Studies*, August 1957, p. 545.

touchable caste groups may begin to play this game in a livelier way themselves.

There appears to be at least one example of an Untouchable group breaking out of its pit this way, the case of the Ezhavas in what is now the state of Kerala. A dynamic leader rose among them late in the last century and one group of them began a determined drive to divest themselves of their Untouchability. They fixed a distance (20 paces) that other Untouchables had to keep from *them*. They refused to be called "Harijans" by Gandhi or "Scheduled Castes" by the government. They also entered into bargaining relationships at various periods with the Nairs, the dominant local caste Hindu group, the Christians, who are a third of the state's population, Gandhi's Congress Party, and in more recent years, the Communists. By some accounts [42] the Ezhavas had considerable success across these decades in shifting their status in the society. They are not listed by the government as "Scheduled Caste" and even Srinivas refers to them as "backward"—a very clear distinction as these terms are used in India. If the bare facts are as indicated, these Ezhavas do seem to have made it into touchability. The question is whether other ex-Untouchable groups will be aggressive enough to force the caste Hindus to modify their ways of holding on to their casteism.

Flickering here and there among these thoughts of the future was the gleam of an idea larger than touchability and surviving caste. This was the notion that there was a larger common identity for all to share, an identity called *Indian*. This was a new identity, a nationality born only in 1947 when Indian idependence began amid the mass fratricide and panic

[42] Cf., R. Velayudhan, *Kerala, The Red Rain Land*, New Delhi, 1958, esp. Ch. III.

of the Hindu-Muslim partition. It has not rooted itself very deep in a society still rent and slivered by regional, linguistic, and caste divisions. In 1962, however, when the Chinese Communists invaded India across the high and far mountain passes, there was an almost convulsively patriotic response by great masses of people throughout the country, an almost spasmic outburst of feeling that startled and perhaps even frightened India's leaders. It had nowhere to go and faded so quickly that many began to wonder whether it had ever really been there. But some thought they had glimpsed something new among the multiple layers of region and caste—a mass of people for whom the Indian *nation* had somehow become not only real but something to which they were passionately attached, people, perhaps, whose other group attachments had weakened sufficiently to make the *nation* the principal means of maintaining their connection to others.

Among the ex-Untouchables I met—this was about half a year after the Chinese attack—there was none of this high pitch of emotion or national feeling. But every once in a while there was an occasional opening of each individual's little view, a sudden widening to take in something larger than caste, something called "India." Describing the differences between himself and his father, a young aspiring chemist said:

My father never thought about the development of India, of the world, of the atomic age. He knew nothing about all this, I do know about it. He had no interest in the progress of India, but I read about the problems of this progress every day in the newspaper. He reads no newspapers, he doesn't read anything.

A Class 1 civil servant told me he was seriously considering quitting his highly coveted job because it limited him too much in pursuing his larger interests. He said:

I have it in mind to change. I am interested in the economic and political conditions of India, going from bad to worse with the poor poorer and the rich richer. I would like to regain my freedom of opinion and writing, even if I have to do so at a lesser salary by entering some other kind of work. I want to concern myself about these problems.

The lady Ph.D. we met in the south, trying to identify herself for us, said: "I cannot take refuge in Hinduism or Indian philosophy, for I am really quite skeptical. I cannot really call myself a Hindu." She cast about for a label for herself, and finally she said: "I am an *Indian national,* that's all I am!"

Forty years ago, B. R. Ambedkar went through a series of crises and choices involving these same issues. When he began in the mid-1920's, he stood aloof from the burgeoning struggle for Indian independence. The Untouchables, he thought, had to win religious, political, and human rights for themselves before they could possibly enjoy any larger freedom. His thrusts at Hindu nationalists on this issue were sharp and true. Caste Hindus liked to say that people were not ready for anything as radical as the end of ancient caste practices; why then, he would ask, do they clamor for independence "when the people as a whole were neither prepared for it nor deserved it?" Despite this, he pointed out, Tilak (the first hero of Indian nationalism in the generation before Gandhi's) rose for Indian deliverance. When Ambedkar was criticized for urging an independent militant politics for Untouchables, he retorted: "If Tilak had been born among the Untouchables, he would not have raised the slogan 'Swaraj [self-rule] is my birthright' but the slogan: 'Annihilation of Untouchability is my birthright!' " Caste Hindu nationalists did not find it easy to take up his challenge to those "who raised violent protests against the insulting treatment meted out to Indians in South Africa . . . and at the same time denied human rights to their countrymen and co-religionists in

India." [43] When Ambedkar talked this way, the Congress nationalists called him "traitor." Like others elsewhere who have felt themselves caught in a hopeless web of rejection and oppression, Ambedkar gave thought at times to migration as a way out. "You must abolish your slavery yourselves," he told his people in 1929. "It is disgraceful to live at the cost of one's self-respect, for self-respect is the most vital factor in life. Without it a man is a mere cipher." He suggested that they might migrate "to some better and distant lands" and cited the example of Muslims and others who had gone all the way to Africa.[44] In 1930, the year of one of Gandhi's major civil disobedience campaigns against the British, Ambedkar finally took a stand in favor of an independent India while at the same time demanding adequate safeguards for the Untouchable minority. Facing the British in London at the Round Table Conference that year, Ambedkar spoke for Indian freedom. But back in India, he had his first historic confrontation with Gandhi, and this exchange took place:

AMBEDKAR: Gandhiji, I have no homeland.

GANDHI: You have got a homeland and from reports that have reached me of your work at the Round Table Conference, I know you are a patriot of sterling worth.

AMBEDKAR: You say I have got a homeland, but still I repeat I am without it. How can I call this land my own homeland and this religion my own wherein we are treated worse than cats and dogs, wherein we cannot get water to drink? No self-respecting Untouchable worth the name will be proud of this land. . . . I do not feel sorry for being branded a traitor; the responsibilities of our action lie with the land that dubs me a traitor. . . . If in my endeavor to secure human rights for my people who have been trampled upon in this country for ages, I do any disservice to this

[43] Keer, pp. 80–81.
[44] Keer, p. 127. See also Ambedkar, *What Congress and Gandhi Have Done to the Untouchables*, Chap. VII.

country, it would not be a sin. . . . I have been striving to win human rights for my people without meaning or doing any harm to this country.

There is a footnote to this encounter that sheds considerable light on Gandhi's essential attitude toward Untouchables. Although Ambedkar was by this time a national, even an international figure as a spokesman for the Untouchables, Gandhi, according to his own diarist and biographer, did not think Ambedkar was an Untouchable but "thought he was some Brahmin who took a deep interest in Harijans and therefore talked intemperately." [45]

In the years that followed, Ambedkar veered back and forth in his search for a balance between the priority of his identity as an Untouchable and his commitment to India as an Indian. He served his country as its first Law Minister and as drafter of its Constitution. Although that Constitution "abolished" Untouchability, he despaired of Untouchables ever winning a decent status for themselves so long as they remained Hindus, and he finally took the path of conversion as a way out. But even in this, as we have already suggested, his choice of Buddhism was, in essence, a compromise with his sense of nationality. Ambedkar died leaving all these issues unresolved, all the conflicts unsettled. They continued to hang over those who had followed him and had to try now without his help to choose their own best path. One of these followers, unconvinced that a change of religion was enough of an answer, told me that when he was asked that eternal and infernal question, What are you?, he had chosen his answer:

When anybody asks me, I say: "I belong to this nation, India. I'm an *Indian*." If they persist after that, I say: "Who are you, somebody from the census bureau?" And they keep quiet. I

[45] Cited by Keer, p. 168, from *The Diary of Mahadeo Desai*, I, p. 52.

WAYS OUT   183

suppose they think: "He's an educated Mahar." And if they do,
I am not ashamed. I am proud of this community, it is a fighting
community, an honest community. But I do really *feel* like an
Indian. This is the best answer. I consider myself one with my
country.

As it does for so many Negro Americans, the question remained whether the rest of the people of his country were—
or ever would be—one with him.

POSTSCRIPT

In the ten years that have passed since the making of the inquiry reported in this book, almost everything indicated here about the ex-Untouchables in India has apparently remained much the same, only more so. Their numbers have increased from 65,000,000 to 80,000,000. They are still ex-Untouchables under the law and they still remain Untouchables in fact. A government committee that toured the country to look into the matter concluded in 1969: "To our utter dismay, the Committee found that untouchability is still being practised in virulent form all over India." In 1970 and 1971, the government reported increasing numbers of violent incidents in which members of Untouchables groups figured most commonly as victims. Some of this violence occurred, however, as a result of efforts by Untouchables to assert their legal rights. One such recent episode, reported in April 1973, involved a protest by local sweepers against the beating of one of their number. They went on strike, demanding more energetically enforced reforms. This took place in the "dream city" of Chandigarh, the new city created twenty years ago by the French architect Le Corbusier to be the capital of the Indian Punjab. The dream had plainly remained only architectural; all the old stuff fit readily enough into the new spaces.

Still going on also, it appears, is the slow trickle of conversion of ex-Untouchables to Buddhism, the ultimate step of severance taken by the Untouchable leader Ambedkar shortly before he died in 1956. In March 1973, in the presence of the Dalai Lama, the Tibetan Buddhist leader now living in exile in India, some 2,500 ex-Untouchables took their new vows on a field in New Delhi. Among the 80,000,000 members of the so-called Scheduled Castes in India, the number of converts to Buddhism is now said to be about 2,000,000. The rest remain more or less passively and more or less nominally within the Hindu system; how much more or how much less is one of many old subjects waiting new authors. But for as long as the margins of change remain as narrow as current reports suggest, the material in this book will stand as an introduction to the status of what is numerically the largest and otherwise one of the most complicated of all the minorities which have become so much more visible in so many societies in our time.

H.R.I.

Cambridge, Mass.
August 22, 1973

INDEX